W9-BGA-958

PEARSON ALWAYS LEARNING

Laurence Behrens • Leonard J. Rosen
• Stephen Wilhoit

Advanced Research Writing

Custom Edition for University of Maryland University College

Taken from:
A Sequence for Academic Writing, Fifth Edition
by Laurence Behrens and Leonard J. Rosen

A Brief Guide to Writing from Readings,
Sixth Edition
by Stephen Wilhoit

ISBN 10: 1-256-91290-5
ISBN 13: 978-1-256-91290-3

CONTENTS

Critical Reading and Critique

■ CRITICAL READING

When writing papers in college, you are often called on to respond critically to source materials. Critical reading requires the abilities to both summarize and evaluate a presentation. As you have seen in Chapter 1, a *summary* is a brief restatement in your own words of the content of a passage. An *evaluation* is a more ambitious undertaking. In your college work, you read to gain and *use* new information. But because sources are not equally valid or equally useful, you must learn to distinguish critically among them by evaluating them.

There is no ready-made formula for determining validity. Critical reading and its written equivalent—the *critique*—require discernment, sensitivity, imagination, knowledge of the subject, and above all, willingness to become involved in what you read. These skills are developed only through repeated practice. But you must begin somewhere, and so we recommend you start by posing two broad questions about passages, articles, and books that you read: (1) To what extent does the author succeed in his or her purpose? (2) To what extent do you agree with the author?

Question 1: To What Extent Does the Author Succeed in His or Her Purpose?

All critical reading *begins with an accurate summary.* Before attempting an evaluation, you must be able to locate an author's thesis and identify the selection's content and structure. You must understand the author's *purpose.* Authors write to inform, to persuade, and to entertain. A given piece may be primarily *informative* (a summary of the research on cloning), primarily *persuasive* (an argument on what the government should do to alleviate homelessness), or primarily *entertaining* (a play about the frustrations of young lovers). Or it may be all three (as in John Steinbeck's novel *The Grapes of Wrath,* about migrant workers during the Great Depression). Sometimes authors are not fully conscious of their purpose. Sometimes their purpose changes as they write. Also, multiple purposes can overlap: A piece of writing may need to inform the reader about an issue in order to make a persuasive point. But if the finished piece is coherent, it will have a primary reason for having been written, and it should be apparent that the author is attempting primarily to inform, persuade, or entertain a particular audience. To identify this primary reason—this purpose—is your first job as a critical reader. Your next job is to determine how successful the author has been in achieving this objective.

Where Do We Find Written Critiques?

Here are just a few of the types of writing that involve critique:

ACADEMIC WRITING

- **Research papers** critique sources in order to establish their usefulness.
- **Position papers** stake out a position by critiquing other positions.
- **Book reviews** combine summary with critique.
- **Essay exams** demonstrate understanding of course material by critiquing it.

WORKPLACE WRITING

- **Legal briefs and legal arguments** critique previous arguments made or anticipated by opposing counsel.
- **Business plans and proposals** critique other less cost-effective, efficient, or reasonable approaches.
- **Policy briefs** communicate strengths and weaknesses of policies and legislation through critique.

As a critical reader, you bring various criteria, or standards of judgment, to bear when you read pieces intended to inform, persuade, or entertain.

Writing to Inform

A piece intended to inform will provide definitions, describe or report on a process, recount a story, give historical background, and/or provide facts and figures. An informational piece responds to questions such as:

What (or who) is _____?

How does _____ work?

What is the controversy or problem about?

What happened?

How and why did it happen?

What were the results?

What are the arguments for and against _____?

To the extent that an author answers these and related questions and that the answers are a matter of verifiable record (you could check for accuracy if you had the time and inclination), the selection is intended to inform.

Having identified such an intention, you can organize your response by considering three other criteria: accuracy, significance, and fair interpretation of information.

Evaluating Informative Writing

Accuracy of Information   If you are going to use any of the information presented, you must be satisfied that it is trustworthy. One of your responsibilities as a critical reader, then, is to find out if the information is accurate. This means you should check facts against other sources. Government publications are often good resources for verifying facts about political legislation, population data, crime statistics, and the like. You can also search key terms in library databases and on the Web. Since material on the Web is essentially self-published, however, you must be especially vigilant in assessing its legitimacy. A wealth of useful information is now available on the Internet—as are distorted "facts," unsupported opinion, and hidden agendas.

Significance of Information   One useful question that you can put to a reading is "So what?" In the case of selections that attempt to inform, you may reasonably wonder whether the information makes a difference. What can the reader gain from this information? How is knowledge advanced by the publication of this material? Is the information of importance to you or to others in a particular audience? Why or why not?

Fair Interpretation of Information   At times you will read reports whose sole purpose is to relate raw data or information. In these cases, you will build your response on Question 1, introduced on page 51: To what extent does the author succeed in his or her purpose? More frequently, once an author has presented information, he or she will attempt to evaluate or interpret it—which is only reasonable, since information that has not been evaluated or interpreted is of little use. One of your tasks as a critical reader is to make a distinction between the author's presentation of facts and figures and his or her attempts to evaluate them. Watch for shifts from straightforward descriptions of factual information ("20 percent of the population") to assertions about what this information means ("a *mere* 20 percent of the population"), what its implications are, and so on. Pay attention to whether the logic with which the author connects interpretation with facts is sound. You may find that the information is valuable but the interpretation is not. Perhaps the author's conclusions are not justified. Could you offer a contrary explanation for the same facts? Does more information need to be gathered before firm conclusions can be drawn? Why?

Writing to Persuade

Writing is frequently intended to persuade—that is, to influence the reader's thinking. To make a persuasive case, the writer must begin with an assertion that is arguable, some statement about which reasonable people could disagree. Such an assertion, when it serves as the essential organizing principle of the article or book, is called a *thesis*. Here are two examples:

> Because they do not speak English, many children in this affluent land are being denied their fundamental right to equal educational opportunity.

> Bilingual education, which has been stridently promoted by a small group of activists with their own agenda, is detrimental to the very students it is supposed to serve.

Thesis statements such as these—and the subsequent assertions used to help support them—represent conclusions that authors have drawn as a result of researching and thinking about an issue. You go through the same process yourself when you write persuasive papers or critiques. And just as you are entitled to evaluate critically the assertions of authors you read, so your professors—and other students—are entitled to evaluate *your* assertions, whether they be written arguments or comments made in class discussion.

Keep in mind that writers organize arguments by arranging evidence to support one conclusion and to oppose (or dismiss) another. You can assess the validity of an argument and its conclusion by determining whether the author has (1) clearly defined key terms, (2) used information fairly, and (3) argued logically and not fallaciously (see pp. 58–62).

Exercise 2.1

Informative and Persuasive Thesis Statements

With a partner from your class, identify at least one informative and one persuasive thesis statement from two passages of your own choosing. Photocopy these passages and highlight the statements you have selected.

As an alternative, and also working with a partner, write one informative and one persuasive thesis statement for *three* of the topics listed in the last paragraph of this exercise. For example, for the topic of prayer in schools, your informative thesis statement could read:

> Both advocates and opponents of school prayer frame their position as a matter of freedom.

Your persuasive thesis statement might be worded:

> As long as schools don't dictate what kinds of prayers students should say, then school prayer should be allowed and even encouraged.

Don't worry about taking a position that you agree with or feel you could support; this exercise doesn't require that you write an essay. The topics:

school prayer

gun control

immigration

stem cell research

grammar instruction in English class

violent lyrics in music

teaching computer skills in primary schools

curfews in college dormitories

course registration procedures

Evaluating Persuasive Writing

Read the argument that follows on the cancellation of the National Aeronautics and Space Administration's lunar program. We will illustrate our discussion on defining terms, using information fairly, and arguing logically by referring to Charles Krauthammer's argument, which appeared as an op-ed in the *Washington Post* on July 17, 2009. The model critique that follows these illustrations will be based on this same argument.

THE MOON WE LEFT BEHIND

Charles Krauthammer

Michael Crichton once wrote that if you told a physicist in 1899 that within a hundred years humankind would, among other wonders (nukes, commercial airlines), "travel to the moon, and then lose interest...the physicist would almost certainly pronounce you mad." In 2000, I quoted these lines expressing Crichton's incredulity at America's abandonment of the moon. It is now 2009 and the moon recedes ever further.

Next week marks the 40th anniversary of the first moon landing. We say we will return in 2020. But that promise was made by a previous president, and this president [Obama] has defined himself as the antimatter to George Bush. Moreover, for all of Barack Obama's Kennedyesque qualities, he has expressed none of Kennedy's enthusiasm for human space exploration.

So with the Apollo moon program long gone, and with Constellation,* its supposed successor, still little more than a hope, we remain in retreat from space. Astonishing. After countless millennia of gazing and dreaming, we finally got off the ground at Kitty Hawk in 1903. Within 66 years, a nanosecond in human history, we'd landed on the moon. Then five more landings, 10 more moonwalkers and, in the decades since, nothing.

To be more precise: almost 40 years spent in low Earth orbit studying, well, zero-G nausea and sundry cosmic mysteries. We've done it with the most beautiful, intricate, complicated—and ultimately, hopelessly impractical—machine ever built by man: the space shuttle. We turned this magnificent bird into a truck for hauling goods and people to a tinkertoy we call the international space station, itself created in a fit of post-Cold War internationalist absentmindedness as a place where people of differing nationality can sing "Kumbaya" while weightless.

---

*Constellation was a NASA human spaceflight program designed to develop post–space shuttle vehicles capable of traveling to the moon and perhaps to Mars. Authorized in 2005, the program was canceled by President Obama in 2010.

5   The shuttle is now too dangerous, too fragile and too expensive. Seven more flights and then it is retired, going—like the Spruce Goose* and the Concorde†—into the Museum of Things Too Beautiful and Complicated to Survive.

America's manned space program is in shambles. Fourteen months from today, for the first time since 1962, the United States will be incapable not just of sending a man to the moon but of sending anyone into Earth orbit. We'll be totally grounded. We'll have to beg a ride from the Russians or perhaps even the Chinese.

So what, you say? Don't we have problems here on Earth? Oh, please. Poverty and disease and social ills will always be with us. If we'd waited for them to be rectified before venturing out, we'd still be living in caves.

Yes, we have a financial crisis. No one's asking for a crash Manhattan Project. All we need is sufficient funding from the hundreds of billions being showered from Washington—"stimulus" monies that, unlike Eisenhower's interstate highway system or Kennedy's Apollo program, will leave behind not a trace on our country or our consciousness—to build Constellation and get us back to Earth orbit and the moon a half-century after the original landing.

Why do it? It's not for practicality. We didn't go to the moon to spin off cooling suits and freeze-dried fruit. Any technological return is a bonus, not a reason. We go for the wonder and glory of it. Or, to put it less grandly, for its immense possibilities. We choose to do such things, said JFK, "not because they are easy, but because they are hard." And when you do such magnificently hard things—send sailing a Ferdinand Magellan or a Neil Armstrong—you open new human possibility in ways utterly unpredictable.

10   The greatest example? Who could have predicted that the moon voyages would create the most potent impetus to—and symbol of—environmental consciousness here on Earth: Earthrise, the now iconic Blue Planet photograph brought back by Apollo 8?

Ironically, that new consciousness about the uniqueness and fragility of Earth focused contemporary imagination away from space and back to Earth. We are now deep into that hyper-terrestrial phase, the age of iPod and Facebook, of social networking and eco-consciousness.

But look up from your BlackBerry one night. That is the moon. On it are exactly 12 sets of human footprints—untouched, unchanged, abandoned. For the first time in history, the moon is not just a mystery and a muse, but a nightly rebuke. A vigorous young president once summoned us to this new frontier, calling the voyage "the most hazardous and dangerous and greatest adventure on which man has ever embarked." And so we did it. We came. We saw. Then we retreated.

How could we?

---

*Spruce Goose was the informal name bestowed by critics on the H4 Hercules, a heavy transport aircraft designed and built during World War II by the Hughes Aircraft Company. Built almost entirely of birch (not spruce) because of wartime restrictions on war materials, the aircraft boasted the largest height and wingspan of any aircraft in history. Only one prototype was built, and the aircraft made only one flight, on November 2, 1947. It is currently housed at the Evergreen Aviation Museum in McMinnville, Oregon.

†Admired for its elegant design as well as its speed, the Concorde was a supersonic passenger airliner built by a British-French consortium. It was first flown in 1969, entered service in 1976 (with regular flights to and from London, Paris, Washington, and New York), and was retired in 2003, a casualty of economic pressures. Only twenty Concordes were built.

Exercise 2.2

Critical Reading Practice

Look back at the Critical Reading for Summary box on page 5 of Chapter 1. Use each of the guidelines listed there to examine the essay by Charles Krauthammer. Note in the margins of the selection, or on a separate sheet of paper, the essay's main point, subpoints, and use of examples.

Persuasive Strategies

Clearly Defined Terms   The validity of an argument depends to some degree on how carefully an author has defined key terms. Take the assertion, for example, that American society must be grounded in "family values." Just what do people who use this phrase mean by it? The validity of their argument depends on whether they and their readers agree on a definition of "family values"—as well as what it means to be "grounded in" family values. If an author writes that in the recent past, "America's elites accepted as a matter of course that a free society can sustain itself only through virtue and temperance in the people,"* readers need to know what exactly the author means by "elites" and by "virtue and temperance" before they can assess the validity of the argument. In such cases, the success of the argument—its ability to persuade—hinges on the definition of a term. So, in responding to an argument, be sure you (and the author) are clear on what exactly is being argued. Unless you are, no informed response is possible.

Note that in addition to their *denotative* meaning (their specific or literal meaning), many words carry a *connotative* meaning (their suggestive, associative, or emotional meaning). For example, the denotative meaning of "home" is simply the house or apartment where one lives. But the connotative meaning—with its associations of family, belongingness, refuge, safety, and familiarity—adds a significant emotional component to this literal meaning. (See more on connotation in "Emotionally Loaded Terms," pp. 58–59.)

In the course of his argument, Krauthammer writes of "America's abandonment of the moon" and of the fact that we have "retreated" from lunar exploration. Consider the words "abandon" and "retreat." What do these words mean to you? Look them up in a dictionary for precise definitions (note all possible meanings provided). In what contexts are we most likely to see these words used? What emotional meaning and significance do they generally carry? For example, what do we usually think of people who abandon a marriage or military units that retreat? To what extent does it appear to you that Krauthammer is using these words in accordance with one or more of their dictionary definitions, their denotations? To what extent does the force of his argument also depend upon the power of these words' connotative meanings?

*Charles Murray, "The Coming White Underclass," *Wall Street Journal,* October 20, 1993.

When writing a paper, you will need to decide, like Krauthammer, which terms to define and which you can assume the reader will define in the same way you do. As the writer of a critique, you should identify and discuss any undefined or ambiguous term that might give rise to confusion.

Fair Use of Information   Information is used as evidence in support of arguments. When you encounter such evidence, ask yourself two questions: (1) "Is the information accurate and up to date?" At least a portion of an argument becomes invalid when the information used to support it is wrong or stale. (2) "Has the author cited *representative* information?" The evidence used in an argument must be presented in a spirit of fair play. An author is less than ethical when he presents only the evidence favoring his own views even though he is well aware that contrary evidence exists. For instance, it would be dishonest to argue that an economic recession is imminent and to cite only indicators of economic downturn while ignoring and failing to cite contrary (positive) evidence.

"The Moon We Left Behind" is not an information-heavy essay. The success of the piece turns on the author's powers of persuasion, not on his use of facts and figures. Krauthammer does, however, offer some key facts relating to Project Apollo and the fact that President Obama was not inclined to back a NASA-operated lunar-landing program. And, in fact, Krauthammer's fears were confirmed in February 2010, about six months after he wrote "The Moon We Left Behind," when the president canceled NASA's plans for further manned space exploration flights in favor of government support for commercial space operations.

Logical Argumentation: Avoiding Logical Fallacies

At some point, you'll need to respond to the logic of the argument itself. To be convincing, an argument should be governed by principles of *logic*— clear and orderly thinking. This does *not* mean that an argument cannot be biased. A biased argument—that is, an argument weighted toward one point of view and against others, which is in fact the nature of argument— may be valid as long as it is logically sound.

Let's examine several types of faulty thinking and logical fallacies you will need to watch for.

Emotionally Loaded Terms   Writers sometimes attempt to sway readers by using emotionally charged words. Words with positive connotations (e.g., "family values") are intended to sway readers to the author's point of view; words with negative connotations (e.g., "paying the price") try to sway readers away from an opposing point of view. The fact that an author uses emotionally loaded terms does not necessarily invalidate an argument. Emotional appeals are perfectly legitimate and time-honored modes of persuasion. But in academic writing, which is grounded in logical argumentation, they should not be the *only* means of persuasion. You should be sensitive to *how* emotionally loaded terms are being used. In particular, are they being used deceptively or to hide the essential facts?

We've already noted Krauthammer's use of the emotionally loaded terms "abandonment" and "retreat" when referring to the end of the manned space program. Notice also his use of the term "Kumbaya" in the sentence declaring that the international space station was "created in a fit of post-Cold War internationalist absentmindedness as a place where people of differing nationality can sing 'Kumbaya' while weightless." "Kumbaya" is an African-American spiritual dating from the 1930s, often sung by scouts around campfires. Jeffrey Weiss reports on the dual connotations of this word: "The song was originally associated with human and spiritual unity, closeness and compassion, and it still is, but more recently it is also cited or alluded to in satirical, sarcastic or even cynical ways that suggest blind or false moralizing, hypocrisy, or naively optimistic views of the world and human nature."* Is Krauthammer drawing upon the emotional power of the original meaning or upon the more recent significance of this term? How does his particular use of "Kumbaya" strengthen (or weaken) his argument? What appears to be the difference in his mind between the value of the international space station and the value of returning to the moon? As someone evaluating the essay, you should be alert to this appeal to your emotions and then judge whether or not the appeal is fair and convincing. Above all, you should not let an emotional appeal blind you to shortcomings of logic, ambiguously defined terms, or a misuse of facts.

Ad Hominem Argument In an *ad hominem* argument, the writer rejects opposing views by attacking the person who holds them. By calling opponents names, an author avoids the issue. Consider this excerpt from a political speech:

> I could more easily accept my opponent's plan to increase revenues by collecting on delinquent tax bills if he had paid more than a hundred dollars in state taxes in each of the past three years. But the fact is, he's a millionaire with a millionaire's tax shelters. This man hasn't paid a wooden nickel for the state services he and his family depend on. So I ask you: Is *he* the one to be talking about taxes to *us?*

It could well be that the opponent has paid virtually no state taxes for three years; but this fact has nothing to do with, and is used as a ploy to divert attention from, the merits of a specific proposal for increasing revenues. The proposal is lost in the attack against the man himself, an attack that violates principles of logic. Writers (and speakers) should make their points by citing evidence in support of their views and by challenging contrary evidence.

In "The Moon We Left Behind," Krauthammer's only individual target is President Obama. While he does, at several points, unfavorably compare Obama to Kennedy, he does not do so in an *ad hominem* way. That is, he attacks

---

*Jeffery Weiss, "'Kumbaya': How did a sweet simple song become a mocking metaphor?" *Dallas Morning News.* 12 Nov. 2006.

Obama less for his personal qualities than for his policy decision to close down NASA's manned space program. At most, he laments that Obama "has expressed none of Kennedy's enthusiasm for human space exploration."

Faulty Cause and Effect   The fact that one event precedes another in time does not mean that the first event has caused the second. An example: Fish begin dying by the thousands in a lake near your hometown. An environmental group immediately cites chemical dumping by several manufacturing plants as the cause. But other causes are possible: A disease might have affected the fish; the growth of algae might have contributed to the deaths; or acid rain might be a factor. The origins of an event are usually complex and are not always traceable to a single cause. So you must carefully examine cause-and-effect reasoning when you find a writer using it. In Latin, this fallacy is known as *post hoc, ergo propter hoc* ("after this, therefore because of this").

Toward the end of "The Moon We Left Behind," Krauthammer declares that having turned our "imagination away from space and back to Earth... [w]e are now deep into that hyper-terrestrial phase, the age of iPod and Facebook, of social networking and eco-consciousness." He appears here to be suggesting a pattern of cause and effect: that as a people, we are no longer looking outward but, rather, turning inward; and this shift in our attention and focus has resulted in—or at least is a significant cause of—the death of the manned space program. Questions for a critique might include the following: (1) To what extent do you agree with Krauthammer's premise that we live in an inward-looking, rather than an outward-looking, age and that it is fair to call our present historical period "the age of iPod and Facebook"? (2) To what extent do you agree that because we may live in such an age, the space program no longer enjoys broad public or political support?

Either/Or Reasoning   Either/or reasoning also results from an unwillingness to recognize complexity. If in analyzing a problem an author artificially restricts the range of possible solutions by offering only two courses of action, and then rejects the one that he opposes, he cannot logically argue that the remaining course of action, which he favors, is therefore the only one that makes sense. Usually, several other options (at least) are possible. For whatever reason, the author has chosen to overlook them. As an example,

---

Tone

Tone refers to the overall emotional effect produced by a writer's choice of language. Writers might use especially emphatic words to create a tone: A film reviewer might refer to a "magnificent performance," or a columnist might criticize "sleazeball politics."

(continues)

These are extreme examples of tone; tone can also be more subtle, particularly if the writer makes a special effort *not* to inject emotion into the writing. As we indicated in the section on emotionally loaded terms, the fact that a writer's tone is highly emotional does not necessarily mean that the writer's argument is invalid. Conversely, a neutral tone does not ensure an argument's validity.

Many instructors discourage student writing that projects a highly emotional tone, considering it inappropriate for academic or preprofessional work. (One sure sign of emotion: the exclamation mark, which should be used sparingly.)

suppose you are reading a selection on genetic engineering in which the author builds an argument on the basis of the following:

> Research in gene splicing is at a crossroads: Either scientists will be carefully monitored by civil authorities and their efforts limited to acceptable applications, such as disease control; or, lacking regulatory guidelines, scientists will set their own ethical standards and begin programs in embryonic manipulation that, however well intended, exceed the proper limits of human knowledge.

Certainly, other possibilities for genetic engineering exist beyond the two mentioned here. But the author limits debate by establishing an either/or choice. Such a limitation is artificial and does not allow for complexity. As a critical reader, you need to be on the alert for reasoning based on restrictive, either/or alternatives.

Hasty Generalization   Writers are guilty of hasty generalization when they draw their conclusions from too little evidence or from unrepresentative evidence. To argue that scientists should not proceed with the Human Genome Project because a recent editorial urged that the project be abandoned is to make a hasty generalization. That lone editorial may be unrepresentative of the views of most individuals—both scientists and laypeople—who have studied and written about the matter. To argue that one should never obey authority because Stanley Milgram's Yale University experiments in the 1960s showed the dangers of obedience is to ignore the fact that Milgram's experiments were concerned primarily with obedience to *immoral* authority. The experimental situation was unrepresentative of most routine demands for obedience—for example, to obey a parental rule or to comply with a summons for jury duty—and a conclusion about the malevolence of all authority would be a hasty generalization.

False Analogy   Comparing one person, event, or issue to another may be illuminating, but it can also be confusing or misleading. Differences between the two may be more significant than their similarities, and conclusions drawn from one may not necessarily apply to the other. A candidate for governor or president who argues that her experience as CEO of a major business would make her effective in governing a state or the country is assuming an analogy between the business and the political/civic worlds that does not hold up to examination. Most businesses are hierarchical, or top down: when a CEO issues an order, he or she can expect it to be carried out without argument. But governors and presidents command only their own executive branches. They cannot issue orders to independent legislatures or courts (much less private citizens); they can only attempt to persuade. In this case the implied analogy fails to convince the thoughtful reader or listener.

Begging the Question   To beg the question is to assume as proven fact the very thesis being argued. To assert, for example, that America does not need a new health care delivery system because America currently has the best health care in the world does not prove anything: It merely repeats the claim in different—and equally unproven—words. This fallacy is also known as *circular reasoning.*

Non Sequitur   *Non sequitur* is Latin for "it does not follow"; the term is used to describe a conclusion that does not logically follow from the premise. "Since minorities have made such great strides in the past few decades," a writer may argue, "we no longer need affirmative action programs." Aside from the fact that the premise itself is arguable (*have* minorities made such great strides?), it does not follow that because minorities *may* have made great strides, there is no further need for affirmative action programs.

Oversimplification   Be alert for writers who offer easy solutions to complicated problems. "America's economy will be strong again if we all 'buy American,'" a politician may argue. But the problems of America's economy are complex and cannot be solved by a slogan or a simple change in buying habits. Likewise, a writer who argues that we should ban genetic engineering assumes that simple solutions ("just say no") will be sufficient to deal with the complex moral dilemmas raised by this new technology.

Exercise 2.3

Understanding Logical Fallacies

Make a list of the nine logical fallacies discussed in the preceding section. Briefly define each one in your own words. Then, in a group of three or four classmates, review your definitions and the examples we've provided for each logical fallacy. Collaborate with your group to find or invent additional examples for each of the fallacies. Compare your examples with those generated by the other groups in your class.

Writing to Entertain

Authors write not only to inform and persuade but also to entertain. One response to entertainment is a hearty laugh, but it is possible to entertain without encouraging laughter: A good book or play or poem may prompt you to reflect, grow wistful, become elated, get angry. Laughter is only one of many possible reactions. Like a response to an informative piece or an argument, your response to an essay, poem, story, play, novel, or film should be precisely stated and carefully developed. Ask yourself some of the following questions (you won't have space to explore all of them, but try to consider the most important ones):

- Did I care for the portrayal of a certain character?
- Did that character (or a group of characters united by occupation, age, ethnicity, etc.) seem overly sentimental, for example, or heroic?
- Did his adversaries seem too villainous or stupid?
- Were the situations believable?
- Was the action interesting or merely formulaic?
- Was the theme developed subtly or powerfully, or did the work come across as preachy or unconvincing?
- Did the action at the end of the work follow plausibly from what had come before? Was the language fresh and incisive or stale and predictable?

Explain as specifically as possible what elements of the work seemed effective or ineffective and why. Offer an overall assessment, elaborating on your views.

Question 2: To What Extent Do You Agree with the Author?

A critical evaluation consists of two parts. The first part, just discussed, assesses the accuracy and effectiveness of an argument in terms of the author's logic and use of evidence. The second part, discussed here, responds to the argument—that is, agrees or disagrees with it.

Identify Points of Agreement and Disagreement

Be precise in identifying where you agree and disagree with an author. State as clearly as possible what *you* believe, in relation to what the author believes, as presented in the piece. Whether you agree enthusiastically, agree with reservations, or disagree, you can organize your reactions in two parts:

- Summarize the author's position.
- State your own position and explain why you believe as you do. The elaboration, in effect, becomes an argument itself, and this is true regardless of the position you take.

Any opinion that you express is effective to the extent you support it by supplying evidence from your reading (which should be properly cited), your observation, or your personal experience. Without such evidence, opinions cannot be authoritative. "I thought the article on inflation was lousy." Or: "It was terrific." Why? "I just thought so, that's all." Such opinions have no value because the criticism is imprecise: The critic has taken neither the time to read the article carefully nor the time to carefully explore his or her own reactions.

Exercise 2.4

Exploring Your Viewpoints—in Three Paragraphs

Go to a Web site that presents short persuasive essays on current social issues, such as reason.com, opinion-pages.org, drudgereport.com, or Speakout.com. Or go to an Internet search engine like Google or Bing and type in a social issue together with the word "articles," "editorials," or "opinion," and see what you find. Locate a selection on a topic of interest that takes a clear, argumentative position. Print out the selection on which you choose to focus.

- Write one paragraph summarizing the author's key argument.
- Write two paragraphs articulating your agreement or disagreement with the author. (Devote each paragraph to a *single* point of agreement or disagreement.)

Be sure to explain why you think or feel the way you do and, wherever possible, cite relevant evidence—from your reading, experience, or observation.

Explore the Reasons for Agreement and Disagreement: Evaluate Assumptions

One way of elaborating your reactions to a reading is to explore the underlying *reasons* for agreement and disagreement. Your reactions are based largely on assumptions that you hold and how those assumptions compare with the author's. An *assumption* is a fundamental statement about the world and its operations that you take to be true. Often, a writer will express an assumption directly, as in this example:

> #1 One of government's most important functions is to raise and spend tax revenues on projects that improve the housing, medical, and nutritional needs of its citizens.

In this instance, the writer's claim is a direct expression of a fundamental belief about how the world, or some part of it, should work. The argumentative claim *is* the assumption. Just as often, an argument and its underlying assumption are not identical. In these cases, the assumption is some other statement that is implied by the argumentative claim—as in this example:

> #2 Human spaceflight is a waste of public money.

The logic of this second statement rests on an unstated assumption relating to the word *waste*. What, in this writer's view, is a *waste* of money? What is an effective or justified use? In order to agree or not with statement #2, a critical reader must know what assumption(s) it rests on. A good candidate for such an assumption would be statement #1. That is, a person who believes statement #1 about how governments ought to raise and spend money could well make statement #2. This may not be the only assumption underlying statement #2, but it could well be one of them.

Inferring and Implying Assumptions

Infer and *imply* are keywords relating to hidden, or unstated, assumptions; you should be clear on their meanings. A critical reader *infers* what is hidden in a statement and, through that inference, brings what is hidden into the open for examination. Thus, the critical reader infers from statement #2 on human spaceflight the writer's assumption (statement #1) on how governments should spend money. At the same time, the writer of statement #2 *implies* (hints at but does not state directly) an assumption about how governments should spend money. There will be times when writers make statements and are unaware of their own assumptions.

Assumptions provide the foundation on which entire presentations are built. You may find an author's assumptions invalid—that is, not supported by factual evidence. You may disagree with value-based assumptions underlying an author's position—for instance, what constitutes "good" or "correct" behavior. In both cases, you may well disagree with the conclusions that follow from these assumptions. Alternatively, when you find that your own assumptions are contradicted by actual experience, you may be forced to conclude that certain of your fundamental beliefs about the world and how it works were mistaken.

An Example of Hidden Assumptions from the World of Finance

An interesting example of an assumption fatally colliding with reality was revealed during a recent congressional investigation into the financial meltdown of late 2008 precipitated by the collapse of the home mortgage market—itself precipitated, many believed, by an insufficiently regulated banking and financial system run amuck. During his testimony before the House Oversight Committee in October of that year, former Federal Reserve chairman Alan Greenspan was grilled by committee chairman Henry Waxman (D-CA) about his "ideology"—essentially an assumption or set of assumptions that become a governing principle. (In the following transcript, you can substitute the word "assumption" for "ideology.")

Greenspan responded, "I do have an ideology. My judgment is that free, competitive markets are by far the unrivaled way to organize economies. We have tried regulation; none meaningfully worked." Greenspan defined an ideology as "a conceptual framework [for] the way people deal with reality. Everyone has one. You have to. To exist, you need an ideology." And he pointed out that the assumptions on which he and the Federal Reserve operated were supported by "the best banking lawyers in the business...and an outside counsel of expert professionals to advise on regulatory matters."

Greenspan then admitted that in light of the economic disaster engulfing the nation, he had found a "flaw" in his ideology—that actual experience had violated some of his fundamental beliefs. The testimony continues:

> Chairman Waxman: You found a flaw?
>
> Mr. Greenspan: I found a flaw in the model that I perceived is the critical functioning structure that defines how the world works, so to speak.
>
> Chairman Waxman: In other words, you found that your view of the world, your ideology, was not right, it was not working.
>
> Mr. Greenspan: Precisely. That's precisely the reason I was shocked, because I had been going for 40 years or more with very considerable evidence that it was working exceptionally well.*

The lesson? All the research, expertise, and logical argumentation in the world will fail if the premise (assumption, ideology) on which it is based turns out to be "flawed."

How do you determine the validity of assumptions once you have identified them? In the absence of more scientific criteria, you start by considering how well the author's assumptions stack up against your own experience, observations, reading, and values—while remaining honestly aware of the limits of your own personal knowledge.

Readers will want to examine the assumption at the heart of Krauthammer's essay: that continuing NASA's manned space program and, in particular, the program to return human beings to the moon, is a worthwhile enterprise. The writer of the critique that follows questions this assumption. But you may not: you may instead fully support such a program. That's your decision, perhaps made even *before* you read Krauthammer's essay, perhaps as a *result* of having read it. What you must do as a critical reader is to recognize assumptions, whether they are stated or not. You should spell

*United States. Cong. House Committee on Oversight and Government Reform. *The Financial Crisis and the Role of Federal Regulators.* 110th Cong., 2nd sess. Washington: GPO, 2008.

them out and then accept or reject them. Ultimately, your agreement or disagreement with an author will rest on your agreement or disagreement with that author's assumptions.

■ CRITIQUE

In Chapter 1 we focused on summary—the condensed presentation of ideas from another source. Summary is fundamental to much of academic writing because such writing relies so heavily on the works of others for the support of its claims. It's not going too far to say that summarizing is the critical thinking skill from which a majority of academic writing builds. However, most academic thinking and writing goes beyond summary. Generally, we use summary to restate our understanding of things we see or read. We then put that summary to use. In academic writing, one typical use of summary is as a prelude to critique.

A *critique* is a *formalized, critical reading of a passage*. It is also a personal response; but writing a critique is considerably more rigorous than saying that a movie is "great," or a book is "fascinating," or "I didn't like it." These are all responses, and, as such, they're a valid, even essential, part of your understanding of what you see and read. But such responses don't illuminate the subject—even for you—if you haven't explained how you arrived at your conclusions.

Your task in writing a critique is to turn your critical reading of a passage into a systematic evaluation in order to deepen your reader's (and your own) understanding of that passage. When you read a selection to critique, determine the following:

- What an author says
- How well the points are made
- What assumptions underlie the argument
- What issues are overlooked
- What implications can be drawn from such an analysis

When you write a critique, positive or negative, include the following:

- A fair and accurate summary of the passage
- Information and ideas from other sources (your reading or your personal experience and observations) if you think these are pertinent
- A statement of your agreement or disagreement with the author, backed by specific examples and clear logic
- A clear statement of your own assumptions

Remember that you bring to bear on any subject an entire set of assumptions about the world. Stated or not, these assumptions underlie every evaluative comment you make. You therefore have an obligation, both to the reader and to yourself, to clarify your standards by making your assumptions explicit. Not only do your readers stand to gain by your forthrightness, but you do as well. The process of writing a critical assessment forces you to examine your own knowledge, beliefs, and assumptions. Ultimately, the critique is a way of learning about yourself—yet another example of the ways in which writing is useful as a tool for critical thinking.

How to Write Critiques

You may find it useful to organize a critique into five sections: introduction, summary, assessment of the presentation (on its own terms), your response to the presentation, and conclusion.

The box on pages 68–69 offers guidelines for writing critiques. These guidelines do not constitute a rigid formula. Most professional authors write critiques that do not follow the structure outlined here. Until you are more confident and practiced in writing critiques, however, we suggest you follow these guidelines. They are meant not to restrict you, but rather to provide a workable sequence for writing critiques until a more fully developed set of experiences and authorial instincts are available to guide you.

Guidelines for Writing Critiques

- ***Introduce.*** Introduce both the passage under analysis and the author. State the author's main argument and the point(s) you intend to make about it.

  Provide background material to help your readers understand the relevance or appeal of the passage. This background material might include one or more of the following: an explanation of why the subject is of current interest; a reference to a possible controversy surrounding the subject of the passage or the passage itself; biographical information about the author; an account of the circumstances under which the passage was written; a reference to the intended audience of the passage.

- ***Summarize.*** Summarize the author's main points, making sure to state the author's purpose for writing.

- ***Assess the presentation.*** Evaluate the validity of the author's presentation, distinct from your points of agreement or disagreement. Comment on the author's success in achieving his or her purpose by reviewing three or four specific points. You might base your review on one or more of the following criteria:

  Is the information accurate?

  Is the information significant?

  Has the author defined terms clearly?

  Has the author used and interpreted information fairly?

  Has the author argued logically?

(continues)

> • *Respond to the presentation.* Now it is your turn to respond to the
> author's views. With which views do you agree? With which do you
> disagree? Discuss your reasons for agreement and disagreement,
> when possible tying these reasons to assumptions—both the au-
> thor's and your own. Where necessary, draw on outside sources
> to support your ideas.
>
> • *Conclude.* State your conclusions about the overall validity of the
> piece—your assessment of the author's success at achieving his
> or her aims and your reactions to the author's views. Remind the
> reader of the weaknesses and strengths of the passage.

■ DEMONSTRATION: CRITIQUE

The critique that follows is based on Charles Krauthammer's op-ed
piece "The Moon We Left Behind" (pp. 55–56), which we have already
begun to examine. In this formal critique, you will see that it is possible
to agree with an author's main point, at least provisionally, yet disagree
with other elements of the argument. Critiquing a different selection,
you could just as easily accept the author's facts and figures but reject
the conclusion he draws from them. As long as you carefully articulate
the author's assumptions and your own, explaining in some detail your
agreement and disagreement, the critique is yours to take in whatever
direction you see fit.

Let's summarize the preceding sections by returning to the core questions
that guide critical reading. You will see how, when applied to Charles Krauthammer's argument, they help to set up a critique.

To What Extent Does the Author Succeed in His or Her Purpose?

To answer this question, you will need to know the author's purpose.
Krauthammer wrote "The Moon We Left Behind" to persuade his audience that manned space flight must be supported. He makes his case in
three ways: (1) he attacks the Obama administration's decision to "retreat" from the moon—i.e., to end NASA's manned space program; (2) he
argues for the continuation of this program; and (3) he rebuts criticisms
of the program. He aims to achieve this purpose by unfavorably comparing President Obama to President Kennedy, who challenged the nation
to put a man on the moon within a decade; by arguing that we should
return to the moon for "the wonder and glory of it"; and by challenging the claims that (a) we need first to fix the problems on earth and that
(b) we can't afford such a program. One of the main tasks of the writer of
a critique of Krauthammer is to explain the extent to which Krauthammer
has achieved his purpose.

To What Extent Do You Agree with the Author? Evaluate Assumptions

Krauthammer's argument rests upon two assumptions: (1) it is an essential characteristic of humankind to explore—and going to the moon was a great and worthwhile example of exploration; and (2) inspiring deeds are worth our expense and sacrifice—and thus continuing NASA's manned program and returning to the moon is worth our time, effort, and money. One who critiques Krauthammer must determine the extent to which she or he shares these assumptions. The writer of the model critique does, in fact, share Krauthammer's first assumption while expressing doubt about the second.

One must also determine the persuasiveness of Krauthammer's arguments for returning to the moon, as well as the persuasiveness of his counterarguments to those who claim this program is too impractical and too expensive. The writer of the model critique believes that Krauthammer's arguments are generally persuasive, even (in the conclusion) judging them "compelling." On the other hand, the critique ends on a neutral note—taking into account the problems with Krauthammer's arguments.

Remember that you don't need to agree with an author to believe that he or she has succeeded in his or her purpose. You may well admire how cogently and forcefully an author has argued without necessarily accepting her position. Conversely, you may agree with a particular author while acknowledging that he has not made a very strong case—and perhaps has even made a flawed one—for his point of view. For example, you may heartily approve of the point Krauthammer is making—that the United States should return to the moon. At the same time, you may find problematic the substance of his arguments and/or his strategy for arguing, particularly the dismissive manner in which he refers to the U.S. efforts in space over the last forty years:

> To be more precise: almost 40 years spent in low Earth orbit studying, well, zero-G nausea and sundry cosmic mysteries. We've done it with the most beautiful, intricate, complicated—and ultimately, hopelessly impractical—machine ever built by man: the space shuttle. We turned this magnificent bird into a truck for hauling goods and people to a tinkertoy we call the international space station....

Perhaps you support Krauthammer's position but find his sarcasm distasteful. That said, these two major questions for critical analysis (whether or not the author has been successful in his purpose and the extent to which you agree with the author's assumptions and arguments) are related. You will typically conclude that an author whose arguments have failed to persuade you has not succeeded in her purpose.

The selections you are likely to critique will be those, like Krauthammer's, that argue a specific position. Indeed, every argument you read is an invitation to agree or disagree. It remains only for you to speak up and justify your own position.

MODEL CRITIQUE

Andrew Harlan

Professor Rose Humphreys

Writing 2

11 January 2011

A Critique of Charles Krauthammer's

"The Moon We Left Behind"

In his 1961 State of the Union address, President John F. Kennedy issued a stirring challenge: "that this nation should commit itself to achieving the goal, before this decade is out, of landing a man on the Moon and returning him safely to the Earth." At the time, Kennedy's proposal seemed like science fiction. Even the scientists and engineers of the National Aeronautics and Space Administration (NASA) who were tasked with the job didn't know how to meet Kennedy's goal. Spurred, however, partly by a unified national purpose and partly by competition with the Soviet Union, which had beaten the United States into space with the first artificial satellite in 1957, the Apollo program to land men on the moon was launched. On July 20, 1969 Kennedy's challenge was met when Apollo 11 astronauts Neil Armstrong and Buzz Aldrin landed their lunar module on the Sea of Tranquility.

During the next few years, five more Apollo flights landed on the moon. In all, twelve Americans walked on the lunar surface; some even rode on a 4-wheeled "Rover," a kind of lunar dune buggy. But in December 1972 the Apollo program was cancelled. Since that time, some 40 years ago, humans have frequently returned to space, but none have returned to the moon. In February 2010 President Obama ended NASA's moon program, transferring responsibility for manned space exploration to private industry and re-focusing the government's resources on technological development and innovation. The administration had signaled its intentions earlier, in 2009. In July of that year, in an apparent attempt to rouse public opinion against the President's revised priorities for space exploration, Charles Krauthammer wrote "The Moon We Left Behind." It is these revised priorities that are the focus of his op-ed piece, a lament for the end of lunar exploration and a powerful, if flawed, critique of the administration's decision.

3   Trained as a doctor and a psychiatrist, Charles Krauthammer is a prominent conservative columnist who has won the Pulitzer Prize for his political commentary. Krauthammer begins and ends his op-ed with expressions of dismay and anger at "America's abandonment of the moon." He unfavorably compares the current president, Barack Obama, with the "vigorous young" John F. Kennedy, in terms of their support for manned space exploration. It is inconceivable to Krauthammer that a program that achieved such technical glories and fired the imaginations of millions in so short a span of time has fallen into such decline.

4   Krauthammer anticipates the objections to his plea to keep America competitive in manned space exploration and to return to the moon. We have problems enough on earth, critics will argue. His answer: "If we waited to solve these perennial problems before continuing human progress, we'd still be living in caves." Concerning the expense of continuing the space program, Krauthammer argues that a fraction of the funds being "showered" on the government's stimulus programs (some $1 trillion) would be sufficient to support a viable space program. And as for practicality, he dismisses the idea that we need a practical reason to return to the moon. "We go," he argues, "for the wonder and glory of it. Or, to put it less grandly, for its immense possibilities." Ultimately, Krauthammer urges us to turn away from our mundane preoccupations and look up at the moon where humans once walked. How could Americans have gone so far, he asks, only to retreat?

5   In this opinion piece, Charles Krauthammer offers a powerful, inspiring defense of the American manned space program; and it's hard not to agree with him that our voyages to the moon captured the imagination and admiration of the world and set a new standard for scientific and technical achievement. Ever since that historic day in July 1969, people have been asking, "If we can land a man on the moon, why can't we [fill in your favorite social or political challenge]?" In a way, the fact that going to the

Harlan 3

moon was not especially practical made the achievement even more admira-
ble: we went not for gain but rather to explore the unknown, to show what
human beings, working cooperatively and exercising their powers of reason
and their genius in design and engineering, can accomplish when suffi-
ciently challenged. "We go," Krauthammer reminds us, "for the wonder and
glory of it...for its immense possibilities."

And what's wrong with that? For a relatively brief historical moment,
Americans, and indeed the peoples of the world, came together in pride and
anticipation as Apollo 11 sped toward the moon and, days later, as the lunar module descended to the surface. People collectively held their breaths
after an oxygen tank explosion disabled Apollo 13 on the way to the moon
and as the astronauts and Mission Control guided the spacecraft to a safe
return. A renewed moon program might similarly help to reduce divisions
among people—or at least among Americans—and highlight the reality
that we are all residents of the same planet, with more common interests
(such as protecting the environment) than is often apparent from our perennial conflicts. Krauthammer's praise of lunar exploration and its benefits
is so stirring that many who do not accept his conclusions may share his
disappointment and indignation at its demise.

"The Moon We Left Behind" may actually underestimate the practical
aspects of moon travel. "Any technological return," Krauthammer writes,
"is a bonus, not a reason." But so many valuable bonuses have emerged
from space flight and space exploration that the practical offshoots of lunar
exploration may in fact be a valid reason to return to the moon. For instance,
the technology developed from the special requirements of space travel has
found application in health and medicine (breast cancer detection, laser angi-
oplasty), industrial productivity and manufacturing technology, public safety
(radiation hazard detectors, emergency rescue cutters), and transportation
(studless winter tires, advanced lubricants, aids to school bus design) ("NASA
Spinoffs"). A renewed moon program would also be practical in providing a
huge employment stimulus to the economy. According to the NASA Langley

Harlan 4

Research Center, "At its peak, the Apollo program employed 400,000 people and required the support of over 20,000 industrial firms and universities" ("Apollo Program"). Returning to the moon would create comparable numbers of jobs in aerospace engineering, computer engineering, biology, general engineering, and meteorology, along with hosts of support jobs, from accounting to food service to office automation specialists ("NASA Occupations").

⑧   Krauthammer's emotional call may be stirring, but he dismisses too quickly some of the practical arguments against a renewed moon program. He appears to assume a degree of political will and public support for further lunar exploration that simply does not exist today. First, public support may be lacking—for legitimate reasons. It is not as if with a renewed lunar program we would be pushing boundaries and exploring the unknown: we would not be *going* to the moon; we would be *returning* to the moon. A significant percentage of the public, after considering the matter, may reasonably conclude: "Been there, done that." They may think, correctly or not, that we should set our sights elsewhere rather than collecting more moon rocks or taking additional stunning photographs from the lunar surface. Whatever practical benefits can be derived from going to the moon, many (if not all) have already been achieved. It would not be at all unreasonable for the public, even a public that supports NASA funding, to say, "Let's move on to other goals."

⑨   Second, Krauthammer's argument that poverty and disease and social ills will always be with us is politically flawed. This country faces financial pressures more serious than those at any other time since the Great Depression; and real, painful choices are being made by federal, state, and local officials about how to spend diminished tax dollars. The "vigorous young" JFK, launching the moon program during a time of expansion and prosperity, faced no such restrictions. Krauthammer's dismissal of ongoing poverty and other social ills is not likely to persuade elected representatives who are shuttering libraries, closing fire stations, ending unemployment benefits, and curtailing medical services. Nor will a public that is enduring these cuts be impressed by Krauthammer's call to "wonder and glory." Accurately or not, the public is

Harlan 5

likely to see the matter in terms of choices between a re-funded lunar program (nice, but optional) and renewed jobless benefits (essential). Not many
politicians, in such distressed times, would be willing to go on record by vot-
ing for "nice" over "essential"—not if they wanted to keep their jobs.

(10)   Finally, it's surprising—and philosophically inconsistent—for a conservative like Krauthammer, who believes in a smaller, less free-spending government, to be complaining about the withdrawal of massive government support
for a renewed moon program. After all, the government hasn't banned moon
travel; it has simply turned over such projects to private industry. If lunar exploration and other space flights appear commercially viable, there's nothing to
prevent private companies and corporations from pursuing their own programs.

(11)   In "The Moon We Left Behind," Charles Krauthammer stirs the emotions with his call for the United States to return to the moon; and, in
terms of practical spinoffs, such a return could benefit this country in
many ways. Krauthammer's argument is compelling, even if he too easily
discounts the financial and political problems that will pose real obstacles
to a renewed lunar program. Ultimately, what one thinks of Krauthammer's
call to renew moon exploration depends on how one defines the human
enterprise and the purpose of collective agreement and collective effort—
what we call "government." To what extent should this purpose be to solve
problems in the here and now? To what extent should it be to inquire and
to push against the boundaries for the sake of discovery and exploration, to
learn more about who we are and about the nature of our universe? There
have always been competing demands on national budgets and more than
enough problems to justify spending every tax dollar on problems of poverty, social justice, crime, education, national security, and the like. Krauthammer argues that if we are to remain true to our spirit of inquiry, we
cannot ignore the investigation of space because scientific and technological progress is also a human responsibility. He argues that we can—indeed,
we must—do both: look to our needs here at home and also dream and
explore. But the public may not find his argument convincing.

Harlan 6

"Apollo Program." *Apollo Program HSF*. National Aeronautics and Space
      Administration, 2 July 2009. Web. 16 Sept. 2010.

Harwood, William. "Obama Kills Moon Program, Endorses Commercial Space."
      Spaceflight Now. Spaceflight Now, 1 Feb. 2010. Web. 13 Sept. 2010.

Kennedy, John F. "Rice University Speech." 12 Sept. 1962. *Public Papers
      of the Presidents of the United States*. Vol. 1., 1962. 669–70. Print.

---. "Special Message to the Congress on Urgent National Needs." *John F.
      Kennedy Presidential Library and Museum*. John F. Kennedy Presiden-
      tial Library and Museum, 25 May 1961. Web. 14 Sept. 2010.

Krauthammer, Charles. "The Moon We Left Behind." *Washington Post*
      17 July 2009: A17. Print.

"NASA Occupations." *Nasajobsoccupations*. National Aeronautics and
      Space Administration, 28 July 2009. Web. 12 Sept. 2010.

"NASA Spinoffs: Bringing Space Down to Earth." *The Ultimate Space Place*.
      National Aeronautics and Space Administration, 2 Feb. 2004. Web.
      18 Sept. 2010.

Exercise 2.5

Informal Critique of the Model Critique

Before reading our analysis of this model critique, write your own informal response to it. What are its strengths and weaknesses? To what extent does the critique follow the general Guidelines for Writing Critiques that we outlined on pages 68–69? To the extent that it varies from the guidelines, speculate on why. Jot down ideas for a critique that takes a different approach to Krauthammer's op-ed.

Critical Reading for Critique

- *Use the tips from Critical Reading for Summary on page 5.* Remember to examine the context; note the title and subtitle; identify the main point; identify the subpoints; break the reading into sections;

(continues)

distinguish between points, examples, and counterarguments; watch for transitions within and between paragraphs; and read actively.

- *Establish the writer's primary purpose in writing.* Is the piece meant primarily to inform, persuade, or entertain?
- *Evaluate informative writing. Use these criteria (among others):*
  Accuracy of information

  Significance of information

  Fair interpretation of information
- *Evaluate persuasive writing. Use these criteria (among others):*
  Clear definition of terms

  Fair use and interpretation of information

  Logical reasoning
- *Evaluate writing that entertains. Use these criteria (among others):*
  Interesting characters

  Believable action, plot, and situations

  Communication of theme

  Use of language
- *Decide whether you agree or disagree with the writer's ideas, position, or message.* Once you have determined the extent to which an author has achieved his or her purpose, clarify your position in relation to the writer's.

The Strategy of the Critique

- Paragraphs 1 and 2 of the model critique introduce the topic. They provide a context by way of a historical review of America's lunar-exploration program from 1962 to 1972, leading up to the president's decision to scrub plans for a return to the moon. The two-paragraph introduction also provides a context for Krauthammer's—and the world's—admiration for the stunning achievement of the Apollo program. The second paragraph ends with the thesis of the critique, the writer's overall assessment of Krauthammer's essay.
- Paragraphs 3–4 introduce Krauthammer and summarize his arguments.
  - Paragraph 3 provides biographical information about Krauthammer and describes his disappointment and indignation at "America's abandonment of the moon."
  - Paragraph 4 treats Krauthammer's anticipated objections to the continuation of the manned space program and rebuttals to these objections.

- Paragraphs 5, 6, and 7 support Krauthammer's argument.
  - Paragraphs 5 and 6 begin the writer's evaluation, focusing on the reasons that Krauthammer finds so much to admire in the lunar-exploration program. Most notably: it was a stunning technological achievement that brought the people of the world together (if only briefly). The writer shares this admiration.
  - Paragraph 7 indirectly supports Krauthammer by pointing out that even though he downplays the practical benefits of lunar exploration, the space program has yielded numerous practical technological spinoffs.
- Paragraphs 8–10 focus on the problems with Krauthammer's argument.
  - In paragraph 8, the writer points out that there is little public support for returning to the moon, a goal that many people will see as already accomplished and impractical for the immediate future.
  - Paragraph 9 argues that Krauthammer underestimates the degree to which an electorate worried about skyrocketing deficits and high unemployment would object to taxpayer dollars being used to finance huge government spending on a renewed lunar program.
  - Paragraph 10 points out how surprising it is that a conservative like Krauthammer would advocate a government-financed manned space program when the same goal could be accomplished by private enterprise.
- Paragraph 11 concludes the critique, summing up the chief strengths and weaknesses of Krauthammer's argument and pointing out that readers' positions will be determined by their views on the "human enterprise" and the purpose of government. How do we balance our "human responsibility" for the expansion of knowledge and technology with the competing claims of education, poverty, crime, and national security?

WRITING ASSIGNMENT: CRITIQUE

Read and then write a critique of "The Common App Fallacy," in which a columnist for New York University's *Washington Square News* argues against the wisdom of using the Common Application in the college application process. You might read such an essay in your own college newspaper; here is your opportunity to respond. The piece originally appeared in the *Washington Square News* on January 22, 2008.

Before reading, review the tips presented in the Critical Reading for Critique box (pp. 76–77). When you're ready to write your critique, start by jotting down notes in response to the tips for critical reading and the earlier discussions of evaluating writing in this chapter. What assumptions does Damon Beres make? Review the logical fallacies on pages 58–62, and identify any that appear in the essay. Work out your ideas on paper, perhaps producing an outline. Then write a rough draft of your critique. Review the reading and revise your rough draft at least once before considering it finished. You may want to look ahead to Chapter 6, "Writing as a Process," to help guide you through writing your critique.

For an additional exercise in writing critiques, see Chapter 8, a practice chapter that assembles readings on the topic of the changing nature of jobs in a global economy. You will have the opportunity to write a critique that you then place into a larger argument.

THE COMMON APP FALLACY

Damon Beres

It's a small miracle that I'm able to have this column for you today. No, I'm not a victim of crippling arthritis, nor did my sticky laptop keyboard give me carpal tunnel syndrome. Rather, it dawned on me that I was one of over 11,000 chosen from a pool of nearly 34,000 students, as the Office of Undergraduate Admissions reports, to join New York University's freshman class last year. If I were a smarter man, I'd start playing the lottery.

Truth is, college applications are a crapshoot in this day and age. My friends back home, with GPAs that resemble the population of China and extracurriculars that make Jimmy Carter look like a lazy old coot, are getting shut out of the Ivies, shut out of their "targets," and, well, shut out of everywhere. At this rate, it seems the only thing most of them will be getting into is antidepressants.

Colleges nationwide, from Yale University to the University of South Carolina, have been reporting substantial increases in applications for years now. Part of that is good, as that probably means that more kids are interested in pursuing higher education. The downside, of course, is that many aren't getting into the schools they want or deserve.

In order to counter this, students apply to as many schools as they can, spitting applications out like bitter saliva. The average from people I've talked to seems to be around 10, though many that I know have applied to upward of 16. What they don't seem to realize is that hedging their bets like this is only making things worse for everyone. Schools have a larger, more competitive application pool to pick from, and kids are taking spots at universities that they may, in fact, have little to no interest in.

5   It's not their fault, though; universities, the College Board, and worst of all, the Common Application are encouraging this dance. The College Board makes it easy to blast those precious SAT scores out to every college under the sun, provided mommy and daddy's credit card isn't maxed out, while the Common Application makes shuttling apps to any number of schools a simple process of point-and-click. With such tools at their disposal, and knowing that the competition will make full use of them, how could any student resist mass applications?

As the nation's top "dream school," as reported by the *Princeton Review* (and why not? We've had Olsens, an Osment and that little girl from *Matilda*), NYU is in a prime position to affect the application process. Harvard caused quite a stir when it got rid of early admissions, so why won't NYU's admissions department do something similar and become a nationwide trendsetter?

It's simple, really: Get rid of the Common Application. Besides pulling in easy money from application fees, what benefit does it provide? New York University is already a competitive institution, a school that's more than able to play in the big leagues, so it certainly doesn't need the extra applicants that the Common App brings in. The more universities that can shake faith in the Common App, the better; it's a cheap, money-making scheme that homogenizes applicants and schools alike. A supplemental essay or two for each school—essays that can easily be adapted from essays for other schools—certainly can't make up for a personalized, unique application that shows a serious interest in the school. It's troubling that nearly 100 universities, including the likes of Dartmouth, Northwestern and Yale, are Common App–exclusive, as it indicates that the college application process has turned from an individualized search for the right place into a cold, sterile business. NYU has a reputation, so why doesn't it use it?

Maybe it has to be a joint endeavor. Maybe high school students should actually care about their applications, which might mean taking the time to search for a handful of schools that they feel are perfect fits. Maybe the College Board and Common App should go all-out with their greed and charge more to send out scores and applications to discourage students from sending them out with reckless abandon. Maybe it doesn't all have to be such a crapshoot.

For the class of 2011, Williams College accepted 1,194 students out of 6,448. Massachusetts Institute of Technology accepted 1,553 out of 12,445. Brown University accepted 2,683 out of 19,059. Princeton University accepted 1,838 out of 18,942. I have about a one-in-five chance of winning on a "Crazy Cash" scratch-off ticket. Shouldn't students have a better chance at getting into college?

Chapter 6

CRITIQUE

DEFINITION AND PURPOSE

While response essays focus on your personal reactions to a reading, critiques offer a more formal evaluation. Instead of responding to a reading in light of your experience and feelings, in a critique you evaluate a source text's quality or worth according to a set of established criteria. Based on your evaluation, you then assert some judgment concerning the text—whether the reading was effective, ineffective, valuable, or trivial. Critiques, then, are usually argumentative. Your goal is to convince your readers to accept your judgments concerning the quality of the reading.

These judgments will be based on certain criteria and standards. **Criteria** are certain aspects of a reading that serve as the basis of your assessment—for example, the text's style or use of evidence. **Standards** serve as the basis for evaluating a criterion—what makes a certain "style" good or bad, acceptable or unacceptable? What counts as "valid" evidence in a reading? When you critique a reading, you will employ either **general** academic criteria and standards (those used to evaluate source material in many fields) or **discipline-specific** criteria and standards (those used by scholars in a particular field of study and generally not applicable to material studied in other disciplines).

In college composition courses you may learn how to critique a source text using general evaluative criteria—for example, how to assess the quality of a reading based on its structure, style, or evidence. These criteria can help you evaluate source material in a variety of classes. In your other college courses you may learn discipline-specific evaluative criteria typically used to assess source material in that field of study. For example, in an English literature course you may learn the criteria used by scholars to critique a poem or a play; in an accounting class, you may learn to employ the criteria and standards experts in that discipline use to critique a financial report or prospectus.

Students often find the idea of writing a critique intimidating: they are not sure what the assignment is asking them to do, how to generate material for their paper, what to include in their essay, how to support their assertions, or what tone to assume. However, you are probably more familiar with this type of writing than you realize since you are often exposed to one special form of critique: the movie review. If you ever listened to movie critics argue over a film, you are familiar with the basic structure of a critique. If you ever discussed the strengths and weaknesses of a movie and tried to get a friend to go see it (or to avoid it), then you have already engaged in critique. Examining how a film critic writes a review of a movie can help you understand how to write a critique of a reading.

THE FILM REVIEW AS CRITIQUE

First, consider the nature of a movie critic's job: he watches a film, analyzes and evaluates what he sees, forms some judgment based on that analysis and evaluation, then writes his review, trying to clarify and defend his judgments with specific references to the film and clear explanations of his assertions. In writing his review, the critic does not address every aspect of the film; he addresses only those aspects of the movie that best support his judgment of it. If, for instance, he thought a film was wonderful, he would address in his review only the aspects of the film that, in his opinion, made it exceptional—for example, the direction, the photography, and the acting. If he thought the film was uneven—some parts good, other parts weak—he would offer in his review examples of what made the film effective (maybe the plot or the lighting) and examples of what made it ineffective (maybe the musical score and the special effects).

Think about the way you discuss a film with someone. Maybe the conversation runs something like this:

"So, did you like the movie?"

"Yeah, pretty much. I wasn't too sure about some of the dialogue—sounded pretty lame sometimes—but the special effects were good and the acting was ok."

"The acting was just 'ok'? What didn't you like? I thought the acting was great."

"Well, there was that scene early in the film, right before he shot the guy; I just didn't buy it when he . . ."

In this conversation, one friend asserts a position about the film, is challenged, then begins to defend or explain her view. To convince her friend to accept her judgment, she will likely discuss specific aspects of the film she believes best illustrate her views.

Most of us are accustomed to talking about movies, television shows, or CDs this way—we form and defend judgments about what we see, hear, and read all the time. However, we are usually more comfortable evaluating movies than we are critiquing arguments, book chapters, or lab reports. First, when it comes to movies, we are probably familiar with many of the source texts—we have seen lots of films—and most of us feel we can knowledgeably discuss what we have seen. We can generate, fairly easily, lots of examples from a movie to support our views. Second, we know *how* to talk about films: we know how to identify and discuss particular aspects of a movie—certain criteria—that influence our judgment. We know that when we analyze a movie we can address the dialogue, the acting, the special effects, and so forth. Finally, we know the standards usually applied to evaluate various aspects of a film; we know what passes for good dialogue, good acting, good special effects, and so on. In short, when we discuss a movie, we know how to *analyze* it (what parts to focus on for review), *evaluate* it (what kinds of questions to ask of each part when assessing its quality), and *defend* our assertions (how to examine specific scenes from the film that support our judgments).

These are the same basic skills you employ to critique readings in college. To critique readings, you need to engage in:

- *Analysis*—break readings down into their essential parts.
- *Evaluation*—assess the quality of those various parts.
- *Explanation*—link your judgments to specific aspects of the readings and make those connections clear and convincing to your reader.

Even though you have probably engaged in this process quite often when discussing movies or television shows, you may have a hard time using these skills to critique readings. First, you are probably less familiar with how critiques look and sound than you are with how movie reviews look and sound. When you are assigned to write a critique, no model may come to mind. Second, the readings you are asked to critique in college can be hard to understand. You cannot critique a reading until you are certain you know what it has to say. Finally, you are probably less familiar with the criteria and standards used in college to analyze and critique readings than you are with the criteria and standards used to review films. When you are asked to critique a philosophical essay on the nature of knowledge, do you know how to break that reading down into its key parts and what kinds of questions to ask of each part to determine its quality? When asked to critique a chapter of your history book, do you know what to look for, what questions to ask? Learning how to critique readings such as these is a central goal of your college education, a skill you will obtain through practice in many different disciplines.

Examining how a movie critic organizes a review can also help you understand how to structure a critique. For example, a critic typically opens her review with a "thesis" that captures her overall assessment of the film. This thesis may take the form of a statement early in the review, a graphic placed beside the review—for example, five stars or two stars—or frequently a comment at the end of the review. Sometimes the critic will love the film; she will give it five stars and a rave review. Sometimes she will hate the movie; she will give it one star and a terrible review. Still other times she will have a split decision; she will give it two and a half stars and in her review acknowledge the strengths and weaknesses of the movie. Next, the critic will typically offer a brief summary of the film so her readers can follow what she has to say in the review. Then, in the body of the review, she will address only the aspects of the film that best illustrate or defend her thesis: she will introduce a particular element of the film (for example, the special effects), comment on its quality (claim they were especially effective), describe a specific example or two from the film (perhaps the climactic battle scene), and explain how that specific example illustrates or supports her judgment (what made the special effects in that battle scene especially good).

Writing a critique involves much the same process. After reading the text, you'll form a judgment of its quality or worth based on some set of criteria and standards. This judgment will form the thesis of your critique, which you will explain or defend in the body of your essay, with specific references to the reading. As you draft your thesis, keep in mind the range of judgments open to the film critic. To critique a reading does not necessarily mean only to criticize it. If you honestly think a reading is weak, based on your evaluation of its various parts, then say so in your thesis. If, however, you think the writing is quite strong, say that. If your judgments fall somewhere in the middle—some parts are strong while others are weak—reflect *that* in your thesis. Your thesis should reflect your carefully considered opinion of the reading's overall quality or worth, whatever that judgment may be.

Next, you will offer a brief summary of the text so your reader can follow what you later have to say about the piece. In the body of your critique, you will choose for examination only the parts of the reading that best illustrate or defend your thesis: you will introduce a particular aspect of the reading (for example, its use of statistical evidence), describe a specific example or two from the reading (perhaps the way statistics are used to support the author's second argument), and explain how that specific example illustrates or supports your judgment (what makes the statistical evidence especially compelling in this section of the text).

Your goal, then, in writing a critique mirrors in many ways the goal you would have in writing a movie review. Your task is to analyze and evaluate a reading according to a set of established criteria and standards, pass judgment on the reading's quality or worth, then assert, explain, and defend that judgment with specific references to the reading.

WRITING A CRITIQUE

Writing a critique typically involves five steps:

1. Read and annotate the text.
2. Analyze and evaluate the piece: break it down into its primary parts and judge the quality of each part.
3. Write your thesis and decide which aspects of the reading you will focus on in your essay.
4. Compose your rough draft.
5. Rewrite your critique.

This is only a general guide. Throughout college you will learn much more specific, specialized ways to critique readings.

STEP 1—CAREFULLY READ AND ANNOTATE THE SOURCE TEXT

Before you start to write a critique, you first need to develop a clear under-standing of the reading you are about to analyze and evaluate. The material you read in college is often challenging; you have to work hard to understand exactly what the author is asserting. However, this work is unavoidable; it makes little sense to evaluate a piece of writing when you are not completely sure what point the author is attempting to make. As you annotate a reading for a critique, keep in mind the following suggestions.

Note the Author's Thesis, Primary Assertions, and Primary Means of Support

Be sure that you mark the author's thesis, highlight and summarize each major point the author makes, and highlight and summarize how the author sup-ports each idea, argument, or finding. Are the thesis and primary assertions clearly stated? Does the thesis direct the development of the paper? Are the assertions supported?

Note the Author's Use of Graphics, Headings, and Subheadings

What graphics does the author provide? What is their function? How do the headings and subheadings organize the piece? Are the headings and graphics effective? How so?

Note the Author's Diction and Word Choice

Consider the kind of language the writer is employing. Is it formal or informal? Is it overly technical? Is it appropriate? Do you notice any shifts in diction? Are some sections of the text more complicated or jargon laden than others? Note any strengths or weaknesses you see in the author's language.

Note the Author's Tone

What seems to be the author's attitude toward the topic? Is he being serious, comical, or satiric? Does the tone seem appropriate, given the writer's topic and thesis? Are there any places in the text where the tone shifts? Is the shift effective?

Note the Author's Audience

When you finish the piece, determine what the writer seemed to assume about his readers. For example, is the writer addressing someone who knows something about the topic or someone likely reading about it for the first time? Is the author assuming readers agree or disagree with the position being forwarded in the piece? Judging from the content, organization, diction, and tone of the piece, which type of reader would tend to accept the author's position and which would tend to reject it?

Note the Author's Purpose

Decide, in your own mind, the primary aim of the piece. Is the author attempting to entertain, inform, or persuade readers? Where in the text has the author attempted to achieve this aim? How successful are those attempts? Note at the beginning or end of the reading your comments concerning the author's purpose.

Summarize the Piece

After you have read and studied the text, write a brief summary of the piece, either at the end of the reading or on a separate sheet of paper (see Chapter 5 for tips on summarizing a reading).

When you have finished reading, rereading, and annotating the source text, you should have a clear understanding of its content, organization, purpose, and audience. Try to clear up any questions you have about the reading before you attempt to critique it. You want your critique to be based on a thorough and clear understanding of the source text.

STEP 2—ANALYZE AND EVALUATE THE READING

Think back to the process of putting together a movie review. When a movie critic watches a film, she forms a judgment of its quality based on certain things she sees or hears. As she watches the movie, she will examine and judge certain aspects of the film, including its

acting	scenery	lighting
direction	costuming	plot
special effects	dialogue	action
theme	pacing	makeup
cinematography	stunts	music

Her evaluation of these various elements of the film, either positive or negative, will form her overall judgment of the movie—her thesis.

What, then, should you look for when analyzing a reading? What parts of a text should you be isolating for evaluation as you read and reread the piece? In part, the answer depends on the course you are taking: each discipline has generally agreed-on ways of analyzing a reading. As you take courses in anthropology or physical education, you will learn how experts in those fields analyze readings. However, analyzing certain general aspects of a reading can help you better understand material in a wide variety of classes. Regardless of the course you are taking, you might start to analyze a reading by identifying its:

- thesis and primary assertions or findings,
- evidence and reasoning,
- organization, and
- style.

Once you have analyzed a reading, isolating for consideration its essential elements, your next task in writing a critique is to evaluate the quality of each element. Here, writing a critique differs from writing a response essay. In a response essay, your goal is to articulate your personal, subjective reaction to what you have read. In a critique, though, you are expected to evaluate the reading according to an established set of standards. Think about the movie critic's job again. Most reviewers employ similar criteria and standards when evaluating a film. If a reviewer decides to critique the musical score of a film, she knows the types of evaluative questions one usually asks about this aspect of a movie: How did the music contribute to the overall mood of the film? Was it too intrusive? Did it add humor or depth to the scenes? Did it heighten drama? Was it noteworthy because of the performers who recorded it? Her answers to these questions will lead to her final assessment of this particular aspect of the film. (Of course, another reviewer employing the same criteria and applying the same standards could come to a different judgment concerning the quality of the music in the film; for example, one reviewer might think it heightened the drama in a particular scene while another might think that it did not.)

In college, you will quickly discover that the criteria and standards used to evaluate readings vary from discipline to discipline. Teachers often employ evaluative criteria unique to their field of study, especially in upper-level courses in which the professor is preparing students to enter a profession. In lower-level courses designed to introduce you to a field of study, you may encounter a different sort of problem. Teachers in different fields may be asking you to employ the same or similar criteria, but their standards are very different. Suppose, for example, you are asked to evaluate the style of a particular reading in both an education and an English course. Your job is the same—determine, stylistically, whether this is a well-written essay. Your answer might be different in each class. According to the stylistic standards advocated by the school of education, you might have before you a well-written essay. According to the standards advocated by the English department, however, the same piece of writing might not fare so well. As always, work closely with your teacher when evaluating a reading to be sure you are applying an appropriate set of criteria and standards.

Below is a series of questions you can ask to begin your analysis and evaluation of a reading's thesis, assertions, evidence, reasoning, organization, and style. The questions are meant to serve only as general guidelines. Your teacher may have much more specific questions he would like you to ask of a reading or evaluative criteria he would like you to employ. Together, analysis and evaluation enable you to critique a reading. After breaking a reading into its essential parts and judging their effectiveness, you will form the thesis of your critique—a judgment of the reading's quality or worth—which you will develop and defend in your essay.

Analyzing and Evaluating a Reading's Thesis and Primary Assertions or Findings

Sometimes identifying an author's thesis can be relatively easy—you can point to a specific sentence or two in the text. Other times, though, an author will not state his thesis. Instead, the thesis is implied: some controlling idea is directing the development of the piece even though the author never puts it into words. If this is the case, you will need to identify and paraphrase this controlling idea yourself and evaluate it as if it were the thesis.

Many times, identifying the author's primary assertions or findings can be easy, too. For example, if the author has made effective use of paragraph breaks, topic sentences, headings, or graphics, you can usually locate his primary assertions fairly easily. However, do not rely on these means alone to identify the author's main ideas. Not every source text is well written. Often, important assertions get buried in an article; key findings may be glossed over. As you analyze a reading, make up your mind about its primary assertions or findings independently of what the author may indicate. Also, be sure to distinguish between primary assertions and their evidence or support. Very often a student will identify as a primary argument of a reading some statistic or quotation that the author is using only as a piece of evidence, something to support the actual assertion he is trying to make. In short, to analyze a reading's thesis and primary assertions, consider the following questions:

- What is the author's thesis? Is it stated or unstated? If stated, highlight it; if unstated, paraphrase it.
- What are the primary assertions in the reading? Highlight each one and paraphrase it in the margin of the text.
- What is the primary means of support offered to illustrate or defend each assertion? Again, highlight this material.

In determining the quality of a reading's thesis and primary assertions or findings, you can begin by questioning their clarity, effectiveness, and organization. The thesis, whether stated or implied, should direct the development of the piece. Each major finding or assertion should be clearly stated and linked to that thesis through the effective use of transitions, repetition of key terms, or headings. To evaluate an author's thesis and findings, you might begin by asking the following questions. If your answers are positive, you can likely claim that the author has effectively presented and developed his thesis; if your answers are negative, be sure to articulate exactly where the problems exist.

- Is the thesis clearly stated? Does it control the organization of the piece? Is it consistently held or does the author shift positions in the essay?
- If the thesis is implied rather than stated, does it still serve to direct the organization of the piece? Are you able to paraphrase a comprehensive thesis on your own, or does the material included in the piece preclude that?
- Are the author's assertions or findings clearly stated?
- Are the author's assertions or findings somehow tied to the thesis?

Analyzing and Evaluating a Reading's Evidence and Reasoning

Here you identify two separate, but related, aspects of a reading: (1) the evidence an author provides to support or illustrate her assertions and (2) the author's reasoning process or line of argument.

First, try to identify the types of **evidence** the author uses to support her thesis. (At this point do not try to evaluate the effectiveness of the evidence—that comes later.) The types of evidence used to support a thesis vary greatly in academic writing, so again be cautious when using these guidelines to analyze the readings in any particular course. However, to begin your analysis of the evidence an author employs, you might try asking yourself this series of questions:

- In supporting her assertions or findings, what kinds of evidence has the author employed? Has the author used any of these forms of evidence:

statistics	empirical data	precedent
expert testimony	emotional appeals	case histories
personal experience	historical analysis	analogies

- Where in the article is each type of evidence employed?
- Is there a pattern? Are certain types of evidence used to support certain types of claims?
- Where has the author combined forms of evidence as a means of support?

Analyzing an author's **reasoning process** is more difficult because it is more abstract. First, you identify how the author uses evidence to support her thesis and how she develops and explains her ideas, her line of reasoning. Second, you examine the assumptions an author makes concerning her topic and readers. As she wrote the piece, which aspects of the text did she decide needed more development than others? Which terms needed clarification? Which argument or explanation needed the most support? In analyzing the author's reasoning process, these are the kinds of questions you might ask:

- In what order are the ideas, arguments, or findings presented?
- What are the logical connections between the major assertions being made in the piece? How does one idea lead to the next?
- What passages in the text explain these connections?
- What assumptions about the topic or the reader is the author making?
- Where in the text are these assumptions articulated, explained, or defended?

Standards used to assess the quality of an author's evidence and reasoning will vary greatly across the disciplines. For example, you might want to determine whether an author offers "adequate" support for his or her thesis. However, what passes for adequate support of a claim will be quite different in an English class from what it will be in a physics course or a statistics course: these fields of study each look at "evidence" and the notion of "adequacy" very differently. In other words, a good general strategy to employ when critiquing a reading is to determine the adequacy of its evidence; however, how that strategy is implemented and what conclusions you reach employing it can vary depending on the course you are taking. Part of learning any subject matter is coming to understand how scholars in that field evaluate evidence; therefore, answer the following questions thoughtfully:

- Does the author support her contentions or findings?
- Is this support adequate? Does the author offer enough evidence to support her contentions?
- Is the evidence authoritative? Does it come from legitimate sources? Is it current?
- Does the author explain *how* the evidence supports or illustrates her assertions?
- Has the author ignored evidence, alternative hypotheses, or alternative explanations for the evidence she offers?
- In developing her position, are there any problems with unstated assumptions? Does the author assume something to be the case that she needs to clarify or defend?
- Are there problems with logical fallacies such as hasty generalizations, false dilemmas, or appeals to false authorities?
- Has the author addressed the ethical implications of her position?
- Is the author's reasoning a notable strength in the piece? Is it clear and convincing?

Your answers to these questions will help you determine whether there are serious problems with the evidence and reasoning employed in the reading.

Analyzing and Evaluating a Reading's Organization

Here you want to identify how the author orders the material contained in the reading. As the author develops a set of findings or ideas, lays out his reasoning for the reader, and offers examples and explanations, what comes first? Second? Third? How has the author attempted to mold these parts into a coherent whole? When analyzing the organization of a reading, you might begin by considering the following questions:

- In what order are the ideas or findings presented?
- How has the author indicated that he is moving from a discussion of one point to the discussion of another point?
- What is the relationship between the thesis of the piece (stated or unstated) and the order in which the assertions or findings are presented?
- How has the author tried to help the reader understand the organization of the reading? Identify where in the text the author has used any of the following to help guide his readers through the text:

headings and subheadings	repetition of key terms
transition words or phrases	repetition of language from the thesis
transition paragraphs	repetition of names or titles

If any aspect of a reading's organization makes it difficult for you to understand the author's message, you may want to examine it in your critique. Clearly explain the nature of the problem and how it damages the reading's effectiveness. Likewise, if the organization is especially strong, if it significantly enhances the reading's clarity or effectiveness, you can point that out in your critique and explain how it helps the text. Here are some questions to consider when evaluating the source text's organization:

- Is there a clear connection between the major assertions of the essay? Does there seem to be some reason why one idea precedes or follows another?
- Are all the assertions clearly related to the overall thesis of the piece?
- Has the author provided headings or subheadings to help readers follow his line of thought? How effective are they?
- Has the author provided adequate transitions to help readers move through the writing and see the logical connection between the assertions he is making? How effective are they?

Analyzing and Evaluating a Reading's Style

Stylistic analysis is a complicated process—an academic specialty in and of itself within the field of English studies. In most of your college courses, though, when analyzing style you will likely focus on issues of clarity and convention. First, when you critique a reading, you might comment on its clarity. You will want to identify which aspects of the writer's word choice and sentence structure help you understand what she has to say or which serve to complicate your reading of the text. Other times, you may ask a different set of questions concerning style, especially in upper-division courses. Your assignment will be to assess how well an author adheres to the stylistic conventions of a discipline. For example, you might explore whether the author's language, tone, and syntax are appropriate for a particular type of writing or field of study. To begin your analysis of style, here are some questions you might ask about a reading:

- What level of diction is the writer employing (how formal is the prose)?

  formal   conversational
  informal   a mixture

  Identify which words or passages lead you to this conclusion.
- What is the tone of the piece (what is the author's apparent attitude toward the topic)?

  serious   satiric   involved
  humorous   angry   detached

  Identify which words or passages lead you to this conclusion.
- What kind of language is used in the piece? Identify any passages using specialized language, emotional language, or jargon.
- What types of sentences are used in the reading?

  simple, compound, complex, complex-compound
  long or short
  active or passive
  a mixture of types

When critiquing a reading's style, you evaluate elements of the author's prose such as diction, tone, word choice, and syntax. Again, stylistic standards vary greatly across the disciplines. While teachers in various disciplines may use similar terms when describing "good" style in writing—that it should be clear and concise, for example—how they define their criteria is likely to vary. Clear and concise writing in a chemistry lab report may have little in common, stylistically, with clear and concise writing in a philosophy research report. Below are some questions that might help you begin to evaluate certain aspects of an author's style. Remember, though, that your answers may well depend on the stylistic standards accepted by a particular discipline:

- How would you characterize the diction of the piece: formal, informal, or somewhere in the middle? Is it consistently maintained? Is it appropriate? Does it contribute to the effectiveness of the piece?
- How would you characterize the tone of the piece? Is it inviting, satiric, or humorous? Is it appropriate, given the topic and intent of the piece? Does the tone enhance or damage the effect of the writing?

- Is the author's word choice clear and effective? Or does the writer rely too heavily on jargon, abstractions, or highly technical terms?
- Is the author's word choice needlessly inflammatory or emotional? Or do the words convey appropriate connotations?
- Are the sentences clearly written? Are any of the sentences so poorly structured that the source is difficult to read and understand?
- Are the sentence types varied? Is the syntax appropriate given the audience and intent of the piece?

STEP 3—WRITE YOUR THESIS AND DECIDE WHICH ASPECTS OF THE READING WILL BE THE FOCUS OF YOUR ESSAY

At this point you need to develop your thesis and decide which aspects of the reading you will use to develop your critique. To formulate your thesis, you need to decide which elements of the source text best illustrate or defend your judgment. You want your reader to understand and accept your thesis, but this acceptance can come about only if you clearly explain each claim you make about the reading and offer convincing examples from the text to illustrate and defend your contentions.

In your critique, you do not need to address every aspect of the source text. Remember how the movie critic supports her assertions about a film. No review addresses every aspect of a movie. Instead, the critic chooses to discuss in her review only those elements of the movie she thinks most clearly and effectively illustrate her judgment. Maybe she will address only the acting and direction, perhaps only the dialogue, plot, and special effects. Perhaps she will choose to mention, only briefly, the costuming and musical score, then concentrate more attention on the film's cinematography.

Follow the same line of thinking when you decide which aspects of the reading to address in your critique. To illustrate and defend your thesis, you may choose to look only at the logic of the piece and its structure. However, you may choose to ignore both of these and concentrate, instead, on the writer's style. Maybe you will decide to look briefly at the evidence the author offers, then concentrate most of your attention on the organization of the piece. Your decisions should be based on two fairly simple questions: (1) Which aspects of the reading most influenced your judgment of its quality and worth? (2) Which aspects will best illustrate and support your thesis? Choose only those aspects of the reading for examination in your critique.

Your thesis in a critique is a brief statement of what you believe to be the overall value or worth of the source text based on your analysis and evaluation of its parts. In stating your thesis, you have several options. You can say only positive things about the reading, only negative things, or some mixture of the two. Your main concern at this point is that your thesis honestly and accurately reflects your judgment.

Also, your thesis statement can be either open or closed. In an open thesis statement, you offer your overall judgment of the piece and nothing else. In a closed thesis statement you offer your judgment and indicate which aspects of the reading you will examine when developing your essay. Below are some sample open and closed thesis statements for a critique—positive, negative, and mixed.

Positive Thesis Statement

Open

> Jones presents a clear, convincing argument in favor of increased funding for the school district.

Closed

> Through his use of precise examples and his accessible style, Jones presents a clear and convincing argument in favor of increased funding for the school district.

Negative Thesis Statement

Open

> Jones's argument in favor of increased funding is not convincing.

Closed

> Due to numerous lapses in reasoning and problems with the organization, Jones's argument in favor of increased funding is not convincing.

Mixed Thesis Statement

Open

> Although uneven in its presentation, Jones's argument in favor of increased funding for the school district is, ultimately, convincing.

Closed

> Even though there are some problems with the organization Jones employs in his report, his use of expert testimony makes his argument for increased funding for the schools convincing.

STEP 4—WRITE YOUR ROUGH DRAFT

While there are many ways to structure a critique, the suggestions that follow can serve as a general guide.

Introductory Section

- Introduce the topic of the reading.
- Give the title of the piece and the name of its author.
- Give your thesis.
- Summarize the source text.

In the opening section of your critique you should introduce the topic of the reading and give your reader its exact title and the full name of its author. You will also include here your thesis and a brief summary of the reading (one or two paragraphs long). The exact order you choose to follow when covering this material is up to you. Some writers like to begin with the summary of the source text before giving their thesis; some prefer to give their thesis first. Overall, though, your introductory section should only be two or three paragraphs long.

Body

- Examine one element of the reading at a time.
- Cite specific examples of this element from the reading.
- Explain your evaluation of each example you offer.

State the Criteria and Your Judgments

In the body of your critique you will explain and defend the judgment you made in your thesis, focusing on one aspect of the reading at a time. Topic sentences in a critique usually indicate the element of the reading you will be examining in that part of the essay and whether you found it to be a strength or liability—for example, "One of the real strengths of the essay is the author's use of emotional language."

Offer Examples

Whatever aspect of the reading you are examining—logic, word choice, structure—give your readers specific examples from the source text to clarify your terms and demonstrate that your judgment is sound. For example, the student who hopes to prove that the author's use of emotional language is one of the reading's strengths will need to quote several examples of language from the text he believes are emotional. Offering only one example might not be convincing; readers might question whether the student isolated for praise or criticism the single occurrence of that element in the text.

Explain Your Judgments

After you have specified the aspect of the reading you are examining in that part of your critique and have offered your readers examples from the text, you will need to explain and defend your judgment. After the student mentioned above cites a few specific examples of the author's emotional language, he will need to explain clearly and convincingly *how* that language strengthens the author's writing. Simply saying it does is not good enough. The student will have to explain how this type of language helps make the author's article clearer or more convincing.

In this section of the critique you will likely develop and explain your unique perspective on the reading. Suppose you and your friend are critiquing the same reading. You could both agree that it is effective and could even choose to focus on the same elements of the reading to defend and illustrate this judgment; for example, you could both choose to focus on the author's use of evidence. The two of you will probably differ, though, in your explanation of how and why the author's use of evidence is strong. You will offer your individual assessments of how the writer effectively employed evidence to support his thesis.

Conclusion

- Wrap up the paper.
- Reassert the thesis.

In your concluding section, try to give your reader a sense of closure. Consider mirroring in your conclusion the strategy you used to open your critique. For example, if you opened your essay with a question, consider closing it by answering that question; if you began with a quotation, end with a quotation; if you opened with a story, finish the story. You might also consider restating your thesis—your overall assessment of the piece—to remind your readers of the judgments you developed in the body of your essay.

STEP 5—REWRITE YOUR CRITIQUE

In rewriting your critique, check to make sure your work is accurate, thorough, organized, and clear.

- *Accurate*—it reflects your true assessment of the source text.
- *Thorough*—you completely explain your assertions.
- *Organized*—readers can easily follow the development of your critique.
- *Clear*—you have explained all the terms you need to explain and supported any assumptions that might reasonably be questioned.

Check for Accuracy

When reviewing your work, first check for accuracy. You want to be sure that your essay reflects your honest assessment of the source text. Starting with your thesis, look through your essay to make sure the assertions you make, the supporting material you employ, and the explanations you offer accurately reflect your point of view.

Check the Development of Your Assertions

Next, make sure you have been thorough in developing your critique. Check to be sure you have offered examples from the source text to support and illustrate your claims and that you have explained your reasoning clearly and completely. Add material—quotations, examples, and explanations—where you think it is needed.

Check the Organization

As you review the organization of your critique, make sure your thesis guides the development of your essay. Are you examining only one aspect of the reading at a time? If not, move material around to improve the organization in your essay. Have you provided adequate transitions to help your reader move through the piece? Do you repeat key terms or provide transition words that remind your reader of your thesis or signal the relationship between the various assertions you make?

Check for Clarity

Check your critique for clarity. Have you used any terms that need to be defined? Have you made any assertions that readers would find unclear? Have you made any assumptions that need to be explained or defended? When necessary, change the content, word choice, or sentence structure of your essay to make your ideas more accessible to your readers.

READINGS

The essay "Zero Tolerance and Student Dress Codes" by Nathan Essex was published in *Principal*. "A Uniform Look," by Yasmine L. Konheim-Kalkstein, appeared in the *American School Board Journal*. Following the readings is a sample critique essay.

Zero Tolerance and Student Dress Codes

Nathan L. Essex

Nathan L. Essex *is a professor of law and president of Southwest Tennessee Community College.*

In recent years, zero-tolerance policies have emerged in public schools as a means of reducing and preventing violence. From their inception, most of these policies were aimed at deterring serious student offenses involving possession of firearms and other weapons, drugs, tobacco, and alcohol.

However, zero-tolerance is taking a different twist in a small Texas school district where over 700 students were suspended in a single month last year for violating a zero-tolerance dress code policy. Under its policy involving student dress, the suburban Duncanville Independent School District in Texas penalizes students in grades 7–12 with a one-day suspension for the first violation, two days for a second violation, and two days plus loss of school privileges for a third violation.

These suspensions, which attracted national attention and threats of lawsuits by parents, raise four fundamental questions:

- How far should school officials go in enforcing zero-tolerance policy relating to student dress?
- Does the student dress in question pose a health or safety hazard?
- Does student dress create material or substantial disruption?
- Is there an educational justification for zero-tolerance dress code restrictions?

There is little debate that school officials are vested with broad and implied powers designed to protect the health and safety of students and maintain a peaceful school environment. Consequently, school officials may promulgate *reasonable* rules and regulations necessary to address health and safety concerns and orderly conduct among students (Essex 2002). A central issue involving zero-tolerance in the Texas district is whether the dress code policy is reasonable. Emphasis on reasonableness centers around the well-established fact that students have protected constitutional rights and that those rights must be weighed against a compelling need to restrict them.

Courts have generally supported the view that school boards have the authority to regulate student dress and appearance if they become so extreme as to interfere with the school's favorable learning atmosphere (Alexander and Alexander 2001). Challenges to dress code enforcement have relied on a number of legal issues, including First Amendment freedom of speech and Fourteenth Amendment rights to due process and liberty. However, the courts have not consistently agreed upon application of these rules regarding dress code enforcement. For example, they have upheld regulations prohibiting excessively tight skirts or pants and skirts more than six inches above the knee, while disallowing regulations prohibiting Freda trousers, tie-dyed clothing, and long skirts.

Justifying Dress Codes

Codes that place restrictions on student dress are not unusual in public schools. However, they must be justified by demonstrating that the students' attire materially or substantially disrupts school operations, infringes on the rights of others, creates health and safety concerns, or focuses too much attention to students' anatomy. According to the *Tinker* ruling, disruption must be viewed as more than a mere desire to avoid the discomfort and unpleasantness that always accompanies an unpopular view or an unidentified fear or apprehension (*Tinker v. Des Moines Independent Community School District*, 393 US 503 at 511.89 S. Ct. 733, 21 L. Ed. 2nd, 731 1969).

However the courts provide broad latitude to school officials on matters involving dress so long as they provide a justification for invoking restrictions. Dress is generally viewed as a form of self-expression reflecting a student's values, background, culture, and personality. Thus, students must be provided opportunities for self-expression within reasonable limits. Student rights regarding dress must be balanced with school officials' responsibility to provide a safe, secure, and orderly educational environment for all students.

Therefore, while students have a responsibility to conform to reasonable dress standards, school officials have a responsibility to ensure that rules do not unduly restrict the personal rights of students. As school officials implement zero-tolerance policies, they are expected to do so in a thoughtful and deliberate fashion, ensuring that their approach is fundamentally fair and legally defensible. Dress codes that do not weigh the severity of the infraction, the student's history of past behavior, the process, and First Amendment rights are at best highly risky.

A Drastic Dress Code

In the Duncanville District, the dress code forbids Capri pants, overalls, sweat pants, athletic jerseys, tank tops, and tube tops. Students are not permitted to wear low-riding, hip-hugging pants or display body piercing. No hats or hooded sweatshirts may be worn. Belts are required unless pants or skirts lack belt loops. Shirts and blouses must be tucked in at all times and should be long enough to stay in. No dress or grooming is permitted that, in the principal's judgment, is "startling, unusual, immodest, disruptive, or brings undue attention to the student's anatomy."

As can be seen, many of these requirements are highly subjective and may create confusion for students. For example, what constitutes unusual or startling dress? School rules should not be so broad and nebulous as to allow for arbitrary and inconsistent interpretation. Fundamental fairness requires that students know precisely what behaviors are required of them by school officials.

It is important to remember that schools must exercise fair and reasonable administrative authority that will withstand court scrutiny. For example, there is a question as to whether the suspension of a 13-year-old honor student for having her shirt untucked was reasonable, even though she immediately tucked it in after she was pulled aside by an administrator. Another student was suspended when her shirt had come untucked when she sat down, and she was not allowed to tuck it back. All students were asked to stand up in their classrooms so that an administrator could determine whether shirts were tucked in and belts worn. If these practices were challenged in court, there would likely be a question of fairness, particularly if no disruption occurred, the student had no history of misbehavior and, did in fact, attempt to conform to the school's policy.

The Key Element: Fairness

School officials should proceed with caution as they develop dress codes, especially those that involve zero-tolerance. Student dress may be restricted if school officials can provide concrete evidence that it communicates a message that appears to invite disruption. However, if student dress does not communicate such a message, school officials must demonstrate a reasonable justification for restrictions. The burden of proof rests with them, although community representatives—parents, community leaders, and citizens—should be involved in the policy development to ensure that it reflects community values and sentiments.

Policies that do not take into account the seriousness of the infraction, the student's record of behavior in school, and the immediate need to act are very risky, as are dress codes that provide no flexibility in enforcement and result in suspension for very minor infractions. When challenged in these cases, the burden will fall on school officials to justify the rules on the basis of past disruption or a legitimately based expectation of disruption.

School officials should always be guided by fundamental fairness and a regard for the individual rights of all students. The Supreme Court's *Tinker v. Des Moines* case reminded all of us that students do not shed their constitutional rights at the schoolhouse door. In formulating dress codes, school officials should demonstrate fairness not because the court requires it, but because it is the right thing to do.

References

Alexander, Kern and David Alexander. *American Public School Law*, 5th ed. Belmont, Calif.: West/Thomson Learning. 2001.

Essex, Nathan. *School Law and Public School: A Practical Guide for School Leaders*, 2nd ed. Boston: Allyn and Bacon. 2002.

A Uniform Look

Yasmine L. Konheim-Kalkstein

Yasmine Konheim-Kalkstein *is a doctoral student in educational psychology at the University of Minnesota.*

Since the 1990s, the practice of having public school students wear uniforms—like their private school peers—has been credited with some amazing results. School uniforms, proponents have said, can lead to improved discipline and classroom behavior, increased school attendance, respect for teachers, better school performance, higher student self-esteem and confidence, lower clothing costs, promotion of group spirit, reduction in social stratification, and lower rates of violence and crime. Uniforms, in short, seem like the solution to all of education's problems.

Of course, there have also been naysayers. They argue that requiring school uniforms violates students' rights, that uniforms are not responsible for decreased violence, that students will find other ways to compete, and that uniforms have no direct bearing on academic achievement.

Which side is correct? Like so many other educational issues, the truth probably lies somewhere between the two extremes. For answers, we can look to the research on and articles about school uniforms, particularly in the areas of violence prevention, school climate, and finances.

Early Signs of Success

Schools have always had dress codes, of course. But in 1986, Baltimore's Cherry Hill Elementary School became the first U.S. public school to adopt a school uniform policy. The policy was an attempt to reduce clothing costs for parents and to help curb social pressures. According to a 1996 issue of *Communicator,* a newsletter published by the National Association of Elementary School Principals, Cherry Hill Principal Geraldine Smallwood reported increased attendance, reduced suspensions, less frequent fighting, increased test scores, and improved school performance after students began wearing uniforms.

A similar success story was reported when, in 1995, Long Beach, Calif., became the first large urban school district to require uniforms for all students in kindergarten through eighth grade. Five years later, overall crime in the school district had dropped by 91 percent. Suspensions were down 90 percent, sex offenses had been reduced by 96 percent, and vandalism had gone down 69 percent.

New York City adopted a policy in 1999 that allowed schools to vote on whether to opt out of a new school uniform policy. About 70 percent of the city's elementary schools adopted school uniforms. In 2000, the Philadelphia School Board unanimously adopted a district-wide policy requiring some type of uniform. That same year, 60 percent of Miami public schools required uniforms, as did 80 percent of public schools in Chicago. Also, 37 state legislatures enacted legislation empowering local districts to determine their own uniform policies.

With so many school districts adopting such policies, it seemed as though uniforms were doing something to prevent violence, improve school climate, or help parents out financially. A look at the research and literature on the effect of school uniforms on these areas is revealing and can help you decide if such a policy would be useful in your district.

Reducing Violence

Proponents suggest that school uniforms can reduce violence in schools by diminishing gang influence and easing competition over clothing as a source of conflict.

In fact, gang violence is one of the most influential reasons for adopting uniform policies. In urban schools, fashion trends are often characterized by gang-related clothing. In theory, then, school uniforms would prevent gang activity by not allowing students to wear gang colors or gang insignia. And in practice, there is some evidence that this is true.

For example, a 1999 *Education World* article by Glori Chaika reported a significant drop in gang violence in Chicago schools that adopted school uniforms. Similarly, in a 2003 *Education and Urban Society* article, Kathleen Wade and Mary Stafford reported that teachers at schools with uniforms perceived lower levels of gang presence than teachers at schools with no uniforms. This difference was significant, despite the fact that the uniform schools were in areas with slightly higher numbers of gang-related crimes. However, students in both types of schools perceived gang presence at the same level. Students may see other signs besides clothing that hint of gang activity.

Clothing has caused other school conflicts as well. After introducing uniforms, the Birmingham, Ala., schools reported a drop in weapon and drug incidents, and Houston schools noted a decrease in violent crime. Interestingly, however, Miami-Dade counties report that fights nearly doubled at their middle schools after schools adopted a uniform policy.

How valid are the findings linking school uniforms to decreased violence? There is substantial criticism on that point. In many of these school districts, other changes in policy were being promoted at the same time—such as having more teachers patrolling the hallways. These additional variables confuse the issue and must be controlled for statistically in the research before drawing conclusions.

Improving School Climate

Obviously, less violence in schools translates to a better school climate, another area that is said to be affected by school uniforms. And indeed, there is some evidence that school uniforms may improve a school's environment by reducing competition, improving student self-esteem, and improving academic achievement.

Writing in the *NASSP Bulletin* in 1997, Richard Murray reported on the results of a survey of 306 middle school students in Charleston, S.C. Murray found that students in a middle school with a uniform policy had a significantly better perception of their school's climate than did students in a school without a uniform policy. Similarly, in Charleston secondary schools, a South Carolina State University doctoral student found in 1996 that a school with a uniform policy reported higher attendance, self-esteem, and academic scores.

Winston Tucker, a University of Minnesota researcher, investigated the perceptions of St. Paul teachers in 1999. He found that in schools where uniforms were worn, teachers perceived more positive behavior and peer interactions. They also reported fewer cliques, less teasing, and better self-esteem. On the other hand, Wade and Stafford's survey of teachers and students revealed no difference between perceptions of school climate in schools with and without uniforms.

Research on school uniforms and test scores is equally mixed. For example, a 1998 study by David Brunsma and Kerry Rockquemore, published in *The Journal of Educational Research*, refuted the belief that uniforms will result in higher test scores. Using data from the National Educational Longitudinal Study of 1988, they found that in Catholic schools, school uniforms had no direct effect on substance abuse, behavioral problems, or attendance. More recently, however, researcher Ann Bodine criticized the inferences drawn from this study. In a 2003 article in the same journal, she contended that examination of public schools shows a positive correlation between uniforms and achievement.

Like the research on a possible relation between school uniforms and reduced violence, findings on uniforms and school climate have yielded no clear conclusion.

Saving Money

Advocates of school uniform policies argue that uniforms will save families money. But Pamela Norum, Robert Weagley, and Marjorie Norton, writing in the *Family and Consumer Sciences Research Journal* in 1998, concluded that families who buy school uniforms spend more on clothing than families who are not required to do so. However, a subsequent paper, presented by Michael Firmin, Suzanne Smith, and Lynsey Perry at the 16th Annual Ethnographic and Qualitative Research in Education Conference, points out that many parents believe a policy requiring school uniforms lowers clothing costs, and others believe it would do so in the long run.

It seems clear that introducing a uniform policy results in more expense in the beginning, but more research is needed to determine whether school uniforms save families money. The experience of families at different socioeconomic levels should be compared, rather than averaging across socioeconomic levels. It is possible that families who struggle financially might depend on hand-me-downs or thrift stores to begin with, and the cost of a new uniform substantially increases their clothing costs.

If a uniform policy is adopted, it will be important to take into account how to provide uniforms for students whose families can't afford them. Some school districts collect outgrown uniforms to distribute to needy families. Some give out donated money so parents themselves can select their children's uniforms. California requires school districts to subsidize the cost of uniforms for low-income students, and the U.S. Department of Education's "Manual on School Uniforms" suggests that some type of assistance should be given to needy families.

In some cases, school uniforms could save money, but it's clear that uniforms could be a financial burden for many families.

Legal Considerations

Legal issues have surrounded the school uniform debate for two primary reasons: claims that the school has infringed on the student's First Amendment right to free expression and claims under the 14th Amendment that the school has violated the student's liberty to control his or her opinion.

The 1998 case of *Canady v. Bossier Parish School Board* addressed the constitutionality of student uniforms. In this landmark case, the Supreme Court upheld a school's right to implement a school uniform policy, given four conditions:

- First, that the school board has the power to make such a policy;
- Second, that the policy promotes a substantial interest of the board;
- Third, that the board does not adopt the policy to censor student expression; and
- Fourth, that the policy's "incidental" restrictions on student expression are not greater than necessary to promote the board's interest.

The American Civil Liberties Union has taken a stance against school uniform policies and cautions schools against omitting an opt-out provision from such policies. "For a public school uniform policy to be legal, it has to have an opt-out provision," wrote the ACLU's Loren Siegel on the organization's website in 1996. "Every child in this country has the right to a public school education, and that right cannot be conditioned upon compliance with a uniform policy. Some parents and children will have religious objections to uniforms. Others won't want to participate for aesthetic reasons."

As we can see, powerful quantitative evidence suggests that uniforms can reduce school violence, but these studies have not accounted for confounding variables. Perceptions of teachers, parents, and administrators seem to strongly support the idea that school climate is affected positively by school uniforms. They have reported more positive learning environments and peer interactions after the introduction of uniform policies. There remains, however, a lack of research on student's perspectives on school uniforms.

The research is not conclusive, but the testimonials from teachers, parents, and administrators alike are hard to ignore. Whether to require school uniforms should be a school or district decision, and guidelines should be followed to make sure students' rights are not violated. That is particularly important in cases where religious practice calls for clothing or head covering that is not consistent with the accepted school uniform. Provision should also be made for those families who can't afford to purchase uniforms.

When these concerns are addressed—and when the idea is supported by the community—school uniforms can be successful.

SAMPLE CRITIQUE

An Unconvincing Argument concerning School Uniforms

As author Yasmine Konheim-Kalkstein notes in the opening line of her essay, "A Uniform Look," over the past few decades schools across the country have debated whether to require high school students to wear uniforms. However, are school uniform requirements effective in meeting their goals: reducing school violence, raising school attendance, bolstering student grades, and reducing the cost of school for parents, just to name a few? On a first reading of the essay, it may appear that Konheim-Kalkstein's goal is to answer these questions impartially by surveying the research published on the topic. However, she withholds her thesis until the last sentence of the piece, revealing her true intention: "When these concerns are addressed—and when the idea is supported by the community—school uniforms can be successful" (119). A close reading of her essay, though, shows that Konheim-Kalkstein fails to support even this assertion.

In the opening section of her essay, Konheim-Kalkstein acknowledges two sides in the debate over the effectiveness of school uniforms, yet she consistently emphasizes arguments and research findings that favor the pro-uniform position. For example, she cites statistics from schools in New Jersey, Long Beach, California, New York City, and Chicago that all demonstrated positive results from requiring elementary school students to wear uniforms and concludes, "With so many school districts adopting such policies, it seemed as though uniforms were doing something to prevent violence, improve school climate, or help parents out financially" (116). Konheim-Kalkstein terms the research on school uniforms "revealing" (116) and states that they can "help you decide if such a policy would be useful in your district" (116). Since this article was published in *American School Board Journal*, one can assume that "you" in the previous sentence refers to school board members.

Indeed, at first glance, the figures Konheim-Kalkstein presents concerning the link between uniform requirements and school violence are impressive. She cites an *Education World* article that reported a drastic drop in gang violence at schools that required uniforms and another article from *Education and Urban Society* that says these results were replicated at other high schools as well. Yet, Konheim-Kalkstein must admit that these statistics may reveal only a correlation between uniform requirements and drops in school violence. She offers no proof that requiring students to wear uniforms actually caused a drop in violence or gang activity; in fact, she states that "other changes in policy were being promoted at the same time—such as having more teachers patrolling the hallways" (117). Any one factor, or any combination of factors, could be responsible for the drop in violence, yet Konheim-Kalkstein wants to attribute it to school uniforms. In fact, from the students' perspective, the uniforms had no effect on violence-related gang activity (117). In the end, Konheim-Kalkstein states that these "additional variables confuse the issue and must be controlled for statistically in the research before drawing conclusions" (117). On this first point—that uniform requirements help reduce gang activity and violence—Konheim-Kalkstein actually offers only testimonial evidence in support of her thesis that "school uniforms can be successful," evidence countered by the experiences of students at those schools.

Konheim-Kalkstein next examines the relationship between uniform requirements and "school climate" (117), indicating some evidence exists that schools requiring student uniforms benefit from reduced competition, higher self-esteem, and higher grades and test scores (117). After citing several studies that reported a link between uniform requirements and better school climates, Konheim-Kalkstein cites only one that showed no such relationship. Moving on to focus on the relationship between uniforms and higher academic achievement, she cites several studies which showed no link between the two, but ends that section of her essay by referring to more recent research that demonstrates "a positive correlation between uniforms and achievement" (118). In the end, though, Konheim-Kalkstein must concede: "Like the research on a possible relation between school uniforms and reduced violence, findings on uniforms and school climate have yielded no clear conclusion" (118). This concession again calls into question Konheim-Kalkstein's thesis, that school uniform policies can be successful.

Konheim-Kalkstein next turns her attention to arguments that requiring school uniforms saves families money by reducing clothing costs for the children. She cites a conference paper in which the authors found that parents "believe" (118) requiring uniforms will save them money in the long run, but again the evidence she examines leads to a different conclusion. A study published in *Family and Consumer Sciences Research Journal* "concluded that families who buy school uniforms spend more on clothing than families who are not required to do so" (118). In fact, Konheim-Kalkstein concludes that school uniform requirements may prove too expensive for students in lower socioeconomic classes. After reviewing all the evidence, Konheim-Kalkstein is forced to admit that "it's clear that uniforms could be a financial burden for many families" (118).

Konheim-Kalkstein closes her essay by examining primarily legal issues involved in requiring students to wear uniforms in school, starting with the Supreme Court case (*Canady v. Bossier Parish School Board*) that affirmed the constitutionality of such programs so long as they met four criteria:

- first, that the school board has the power to make such a policy;
- second, that the policy promotes a substantial interest of the board;
- third, that the board does not adopt the policy to censor student expression; and
- fourth, that the policy's "incidental" restrictions on student expression are not greater than necessary to promote the board's interest. (119)

However, school uniform laws have been opposed by the American Civil Liberties Union (ACLU), which asserts that any school uniform policy must have an "opt out" provision for children and families who believe the requirements inhibit their freedom of religion or free speech, objections that Konheim-Kalkstein does not address (119). American courts have long held that freedom of expression extends to people's clothing, including that of students. Konheim-Kalkstein does not offer a clear position on this question. Instead, she implies that if a school uniform policy meets the four criteria outlined above, it would be legal.

Despite all of the contradictory research and gaps in her argument, Konheim-Kalkstein still wants to maintain that requiring school uniforms "can be successful" (119). To do so, she puts the best possible spin on the evidence she presents in her essay:

> As we can see, powerful quantitative evidence suggests that uniforms can reduce school violence, but these studies have not accounted for confounding variables. Perceptions of teachers, parents, and administrators seem to strongly support the idea that school climate is affected positively by school uniforms. They have reported more positive learning environments and peer interactions after the introduction of uniform policies. (119)

However, these positive assertions can be seriously questioned by the information and arguments Konheim-Kalkstein presents. For example, she provides ample reason to question each of the positive claims she makes for school uniforms, admittedly basing her claim for their efficacy on teacher or parent testimonials (119). Read as a whole, the article actually offers a strong argument against the institution of school uniform policies because there simply is no preponderance of evidence to support any of the benefits such a move is supposed to bring about. Konheim-Kalkstein's "A Uniform Look" casts great doubts on whether school uniform policies can successfully achieve the benefits supporters ascribe to them.

Summary Chart

How to Write a Critique

1. **Carefully read and annotate the source text.**
   - *Read and reread the text.*
   - *Identify the author's intent, thesis, and primary assertions or findings.*
   - *Write an informal summary of the piece.*

2. **Analyze and evaluate the reading, breaking it down into its parts and judging the quality of each element.**

   Identify and evaluate the author's logic and reasoning.
   - *Is the thesis clearly stated, and does it direct the development of the text?*
   - *Are the author's primary assertions reasonable and clearly tied to the thesis?*
   - *Are there problems with logical fallacies?*
   - *Are the author's positions or findings logically presented?*

   Identify and evaluate the text's evidence.
   - *Does the author support his or her assertions or findings?*
   - *Is the support offered adequate to convince readers?*
   - *Is the evidence authoritative?*
   - *Is the evidence current?*
   - *Does the author explain how the evidence supports his or her assertions or findings?*
   - *Has the author ignored evidence or alternative hypotheses?*

   Identify and evaluate the text's organization.
   - *Is there a clear connection between the assertions developed in the essay?*
   - *Are the assertions or findings tied to a guiding thesis?*
   - *Does there seem to be a reason for one assertion following another, or do they seem randomly organized?*

   Identify and evaluate the text's style.
   - *Is the author's diction consistently maintained?*
   - *Is the author's word choice clear and effective?*
   - *Is the author's tone consistent and effective?*
   - *Are the author's sentences clear?*

SUMMARY CHART: HOW TO WRITE A CRITIQUE *(CONTINUED)*

3. **Formulate your thesis and choose the criteria you will include in your essay.**
   - *Draft a thesis, a brief statement concerning the overall value or worth of the source text.*
   - *Choose which elements of the reading you will focus on in your critique.*

4. **Write your rough draft.**
   - *Introduce the topic, source text, and your thesis.*
   - *Establish your evaluative criteria and your judgments of them.*
   - *Offer examples to substantiate each of your criteria and judgments.*
   - *Explain your judgments, clarifying how the examples you provide support your assertions.*

5. **Rewrite your critique.**

   Check to make sure your writing is accurate.
   - *Does your writing honestly reflect your judgment?*
   - *Does your writing misrepresent the author?*

   Check to make sure your writing is thorough.
   - *Do you cover all the aspects of the source text you need to cover?*
   - *Do you clearly and thoroughly explain and support your assertions?*

   Check to make sure your writing is organized.
   - *Does your thesis statement guide the development of your essay?*
   - *Have you provided transitional devices to help lead your reader through your work?*

   Check to make sure your writing is clear.
   - *Is your terminology clear?*
   - *Are your sentences clear?*
   - *Are your examples and explanations clear?*

CRITIQUE REVISION CHECKLIST

	Yes	No
1. Have you included the title of the reading and the author's name in your introduction?	____	____
2. Does your thesis make clear your overall assessment of the reading?	____	____
3. Toward the beginning of your critique, have you provided a brief summary of the reading?	____	____
4. In the body of your critique, do you examine only one element of the reading at a time?	____	____
5. Do you clearly state a judgment concerning each element of the reading you explore?	____	____
6. Do you provide examples from the reading to support and illustrate your judgment of each element you examine?	____	____
7. Do you clearly and thoroughly explain your judgments concerning each example you provide from the reading?	____	____
8. Have you employed proper evaluative criteria and standards?	____	____
9. Have you provided clear transitions between the major sections of your paper?	____	____
10. Is there a clear relationship between each section of your paper and your thesis?	____	____
11. Have you provided proper documentation for all quoted, paraphrased, and summarized material?	____	____
12. Have you revised your paper for accuracy? In other words, does the final draft reflect your honest appraisal of the reading?	____	____
13. Have you reviewed the language in your paper to make sure your words adequately capture and communicate your judgments?	____	____
14. As you review your work, do your judgments still stand? Do you need to change your thesis or any part of your paper?	____	____